Matter
More!

Tom
Hayes

relevance

STYRLUND & HAYES

with DEEGAN

PHIL STYRLUND

To Julie, Kersten, and Hannah—
mattering more to you matters the most to me.

TOM HAYES

To those who have mattered more in my life:
my dear family, cherished friends, and dedicated colleagues.

MARIAN DEEGAN

To Jacqueline Hee, whose gracious introduction
initiated this journey through relevance with Phil and Tom.

TABLE OF CONTENTS

TOM & PHIL

WHO WE ARE; WHY THIS MATTERS TO US.

Thirty years ago, two idealistic 20-something fellows on the brink of our own careers crossed paths while volunteering with a youth group. A grinning—and ganglier—Phil Styrlund struck up a friendship with thoughtful wordsmith Tom Hayes—who then boasted a full head of impressive hair. Our friendship endured through divergent paths in sales and advertising, and as we met through the years over a good bottle of wine to reflect on our own journeys, a kindred spirit was forged. Our successes, we confessed with honest humility as only old friends can, were won as much despite our efforts as because of them. If only we'd known in our 20s the lessons taught to us the hard way, through trial and error. If only we'd started thinking sooner about what it is that really matters.

Phil recounted a conversation he'd had with his father, then in his mid-80s.

Reuben Styrlund was the archetypal Minnesotan full-blooded Swede. He was a good man and a loyal man. He survived the Great Depression. He was among the second wave of reinforcements to land on the beaches of France as part of the Normandy Invasion, fighting in battles that paved the way to the liberation of France and the final invasion of Germany in World War II. He deeply loved Mae Styrlund, his wife of more than 60 years. As he looked back over his long and significant life, Reuben said something that struck Phil to his very core. "It's not dying that scares me," he said. "Not mattering—that's what scares me most."

We live in a world that longs to matter more. Seismic global shifts have made uncertainty seem the one sure bet. Our world is glutted with information yet short on wisdom. The competition to stake a flag on the career path of our dreams grows fiercer, and downsizing can reverse our fortunes in a heartbeat. Security is a myth. It is no wonder we feel like interchangeable commodities. In our heart of hearts, regardless of seductive claims to the contrary, we know that an Ivy League pedigree, the title on our business card, or a regime of Botox® and whitening strips can't make us matter more. As we survey a business landscape, predictable only in its volatility, relevance appears to be the most coveted, elusive, and fleeting prize. In this "post-stability world," the only real security lies in developing a lifelong relevance to those you serve based on your personal gifts and calling.

Our belief is this: relevance matters more than intelligence. As intelligence has become readily available and delivered by myriad technologies, relevance remains a gem of great worth.

Reuben Styrlund's passion to matter more planted a seed that we could not ignore. Over time, the concept of relevance presented itself, and observations and experiences tumbled out of us. Mattering more became the central theme of our conversations. We were galvanized, and we haven't been able to stop talking about relevance since. The conversation has expanded to a circle of our clients, colleagues, and friends. Gradually, it dawned on us that our fascination with mattering more actually mattered to a lot of people. We realized that we needed to delve more deeply into what it meant to matter more in our own lives and in the lives of others. Out of our realization, this project was born.

It is important to us to be honest with you about who we are—and who we are not. We are not gurus, and we know better than to claim mastery alongside the fine minds of Greek philosophers and world leaders and so many others who have addressed the human longing for relevance through the ages. Albert Einstein observed, "The search for truth is more precious than its possession." We couldn't agree more.

We also maintain a simple truth: we are on this planet to serve others. We can't have an impact on others if we are not relevant to them. Elevating relevance is not an exercise in self-aggrandizement—quite the opposite. It is about mattering as much as possible, for as long in life as possible, as deeply as possible, to as many people as possible, in as many ways as possible. Relevance means mattering more to others, for others.

If we are able to offer any insights to you through these pages, they are not the result of our mastery. Rather, they are birthed from our fears, our failures, and our flaws. Based on that, there's much to offer!

We think of ourselves as two guys who are passionate about becoming more deeply confused about more important things. We believe that relevance is one of those important things. We know that we are not alone in our desire to be relevant, and we know that those on the journey with us have wisdom to share. If you are like us in wanting to be relevant, and remain relevant for as long as possible, we welcome you to join us in provoking conversation. Let's talk together about how to matter more.

Phil Styrlund & Tom Hayes
September 2014

SHAKESPEARE HAD A PROBLEM.

He was writing a play about English King Henry V and had come to the Battle of Agincourt—one of the most famous victories in English history.

On the eve of battle, the situation was grim. The English had invaded France at great cost. Dysentery had taken a third of Henry's troops. His retreat had been blocked. He was running out of food. And he faced an army that vastly outnumbered his shaggy soldiers.

Shakespeare and his audience were well aware that the English victory at Agincourt was won by the combination of superior English longbows and muddy terrain. But being the greatest dramatist of his or any other age, Shakespeare knew that longbows would be tough to pull off in the cramped Globe Theatre, and muddy terrain would literally bog down the plot line.

What's a bard to do? Shakespeare hit upon the notion of a stirring speech that would inspire Henry's underdogs to victory. But what words could possibly motivate men to overcome tremendous odds? Fighting to save their families from the French was out—they were the invaders, not the French. The mercilessness of the French toward their conquered wouldn't work—it was true that the French would kill them if they lost, but this prospect was more likely to convince the soldiers to desert than fight. Defending Mother England might motivate noblemen, but would have little appeal for the majority of Henry's peasant army.

Shakespeare disguised Henry and sent him wandering among his troops during the night before the battle. Henry spoke with his men, getting to know their needs, hopes, desires, and most importantly, learning how they felt about their king. Come morning, Henry had his words. He motivated his troops with a very simple thought. The profound insight he had gained was that nothing is more important to the human soul than mattering. His message was as clear as it was inspiring: by fighting this day, his men would matter more for the rest of their lives; this battle would transform them from coarse, lowly peasants into the elevated realm of "gentle men." And from that day forward, they would stand above all those who were back in England in their cozy beds. Of course, our shorthand does not do the Saint Crispin's Day speech justice.

We few, we happy few, we band of brothers;

For he to-day that sheds his blood with me

Shall be my brother; be he ne'er so vile,

This day shall gentle his condition;

And gentlemen in England now abed

Shall think themselves accurs'd they were not here,

And hold their manhoods cheap whiles any speaks

That fought with us upon Saint Crispin's day.

And so our journey begins. To discover how we can achieve true relevance. To live lives that matter more.

INTRODUCTION

Why Relevance?

EXCUSE ME. ARE THOSE RUBY-RED SLIPPERS YOU ARE WEARING?

Utter the phrase "ruby-red slippers," and the mind immediately conjures up a winding yellow brick road, beckoning us forward. The Library of Congress named *The Wizard of Oz* the most-watched motion picture in history; its images are imbedded in our cultural lexicon.

Each generation has imposed its own theories on this iconic film, but we think that the journey subtext is one on which everyone can agree. When Dorothy links arms with her companions and takes her first ruby-red-slippered step onto those yellow bricks, we know that a journey has begun and that adventures await. At some level, we recognize the journey down the yellow brick road as our own. We are each, after all, on a journey—a search for our own unique meaning. Dorothy seeks a way home. The Scarecrow yearns for a brain; the Tin Man, for a heart; the Lion, for courage. Like Dorothy and her friends, each of us hopes for aspiration and determination to lead us to achievement.

The characters define their journey's objective by the qualities they value most highly. Like us, Dorothy and her friends seek relevance through the possession and expression of their gifts.

TAKE YOUR OWN WALK DOWN THE YELLOW BRICK ROAD.

As this Technicolor masterpiece demonstrates, and as personal journeyers discover, the path down the yellow brick road does not always go smoothly. We may be unaware of the resources we carry with us. On some parts of the journey, illusions may lead us to believe that we are more powerful than reality merits. At other times, we find ourselves honing new skills we need to survive and thrive. Occasionally, a humbling blow may shake us from our course and cause us to question the skills obvious to everyone except us. Finally, we discover that when we use our own gifts with empathy to support our fellow travelers on life's journey, the sum of what is created exceeds the individual parts.

The Wizard of Oz teaches us valuable lessons about what makes a journey meaningful. It is not mere possession, but also awareness of our unique gifts that enables us to put them to use. Along the journey, Dorothy and her friends discover not only talents, but also the importance of pooling their resources to support each other. We learn that conquering trepidation and taking that first step is the only way to come to self-awareness, master our talents, and seize opportunities to support each other to success.

We believe in the journey of self-discovery and service that the yellow brick road represents. Our aspirations, like those of Dorothy and her troupe, reflect our innate desire to create relevance in our lives and to seek to serve others in a way that is relevant to them. We each carry with us unique gifts, recognized and unrecognized. We long to harness those gifts in a way that gives life significance and helps us to matter more in the lives of others.

THE THREE DIMENSIONS OF MATTERING MORE.

Along the journey, we view success, significance, and relevance as three distinct but interrelated objectives.

- **Success reflects our achievements and the recognition we receive as the result of applying the gifts and skills we have mastered.**

- **Significance is defined as going as far as we can toward the purpose we've defined for our life with the resources we've been given. It reflects internal perspective: who I am, what matters to me, and what I do.**

- **Relevance pushes our impact beyond our inner self, engaging the world's external perspective of our individual significance.**

Our relevance is determined by how the world sees who we are and how we matter to others. Relevance trumps intelligence. In a world where we are drowning in information but starving for wisdom, relevance is not a matter of what we know; it is a matter of how what we know matters to someone else.

This has been a life-changing definition for us.

COMMODITIZATION: THE FORCE THAT IS NOT WITH YOU.

As we talk with leaders of businesses about their hopes and fears along life's journey, we sense a frustration that brings to mind a scene from another movie, the defining film of our own youths: *Star Wars*. The *Star Wars* scene that keeps coming back to us is one in which Luke, Han, Chewie, and Princess Leia slide down into a giant garbage compactor. Trapped amid the trash and sewage, they feel the walls begin to close in on them. Making a bad situation worse, a giant, mysterious, one-eyed creature is poised to pull them deep into the sewage before the walls have a chance to crush them.

Three aspects of this scene recur in our conversations with colleagues and clients. One is a sense of gnawing fear that we are struggling in a sea of meaningless garbage that eclipses our relevance. There is concern that widespread mediocrity is strangling meaning. Second, we are troubled by indications that our world is becoming filled with the inconsequential. The walls of triviality close around us, indifferent to the unique and distinctive aspects of self that we struggle to express. We fear that they will likely crush us in the end. And finally, as we struggle against these forces, we feel our days and months and years slipping away, and worry that a malevolent event or entity may take us down before our time.

In both of our businesses, we see the creep of commoditization—and it does not stop with products. People, too, are being downsized, rightsized, and commoditized. We see global workforces turning into interchangeable human cogs. The angst of 20-somethings and baby boomers alike is that security is a myth. People fear sliding into irrelevance. We worry that unpredictable economic sea changes will best us before we figure out how to adapt. As stress takes its toll and the inevitabilities of age creep toward us, we worry that our bodies may betray us before our time. Business people, and the businesses they serve, feel like mere commodities, where the only factor that matters is price.

Commoditization is the enemy of meaning. In ages dominated by the forces of commoditization, individuals pay the price with devalued lives. Today, skills have become the target of commoditization. When a skill like assembly-line work or rote customer service is mutually interchangeable, it can easily be digitized and transferred to lower-wage locations; it is fungible. By contrast, unique skills requiring mastery and expertise, like the skills of a brain surgeon, are nonfungible, and therefore safe from the threat of commoditization. We need look no further than North Korea, China, or Wal-Mart to recognize the forces of commoditization at play. Unless individuals have the power to defy commoditization and define their own lives, their potential is vulnerable to the crushing forces of objectification.

RELEVANCE IS THE ANSWER.

We believe that there is a yellow brick road out of the fungible forest—a way to elude the crush of mediocrity. As two Midwestern guys working in marketing and sales, we've grappled with remaining relevant in a world pressured by commoditization. It is our job to fight the forces of commoditization and irrelevance and to help our clients matter more to their customers. We have created methods to distinguish ourselves, and our clients, from the masses.

Over time, by working together, sharing insights, and enhancing our respective skills, we have developed a whole toolbox of strategies and tactics that can make a real difference for our clients—in both their professional and personal lives. We have successfully helped them navigate challenging times, transcend the ordinary, and find a voice that lets the world know why they are extraordinary.

Is relevance a concept for business success or personal growth? Yes. We don't experience our professional and personal lives as separate worlds; for us, they are intertwined and holistic. The principles of relevance apply whether we are having a conversation with a life partner or a business partner. In both cases, being interested in discovering unmet needs is going to help us to matter more. Today's world is not compartmentalized, and the principles of relevance can help us in "the business of life."

Our approach draws from the wisdom of the past and the best thinking of today. Because we have conversations with clients around the globe, we work to crystallize the zeitgeist of the age and the best thinking of the day into insights to help clients succeed. We feel that we have a fundamental imperative in our lives to matter to others, to serve others, and to support each other in mattering more.

YOU CAN MATTER MORE.

We have created a framework for people and companies to become more relevant in their lives and marketplace. We wrote this book to share the tools that we have developed. We believe that relevance is attainable—further, we believe that using the tools we have developed to help realize relevance in companies, in business, and in personal lives may be the best shot we have at attaining security in an insecure world. Relevance is the fuel of significance.

LESSONS LEARNED.

There's one thing we want to make clear: we know that there's no one-fits-all solution that will make us relevant. We love how some modern business books and motivational speakers seek to create simple formulas for success. Do this, then do that, add another thing, subtract your age from your IQ, divide it by the number of chairs in your conference room and TA-DA! You will be a success!

Too frequently, business gurus communicate ideas and concepts that they truly believe—but that don't correspond to reality. It's fine to claim that your techniques are based on research, but when the research consists of anecdotes and small sampling surveys, it doesn't carry much scientific validity. It is also true that we can selectively present research to validate almost any perspective.

Even when we study best practices in one successful company, that doesn't mean that these practices will work equally well in another company. Successful practices may be portable, but they are also contextual in application. Organizations and sales environments are idiosyncratic; this is what unique branding is all about, and there isn't one cookie-cutter approach that will work for every company. Motivational approaches may be entertaining, but we know that motivation is a disciplined choice made by individuals, not a party favor to be handed out in an afternoon.

For us, the path to relevance has been paved with hard work. Phil often recalls his father's words: "They call it 'work' because the word 'rest' is already taken."

We came to realize that if we were going to survive and flourish in the instability of our current global market, we had better quit looking for others to save us, roll up our sleeves, and start saving ourselves.

Don't misunderstand; we aren't saying that formulas are useless—quite the contrary. Formulas can create a shorthand reference that makes valuable tools memorable and accessible. Stephen Covey's Seven Habits formula for attaining goals took the business world by storm precisely because it was so powerfully effective in creating personal change.

It's one thing for a formula to sound good; it's something else entirely for a formula to work—to significant effect—in the real world. We were drawn to Einstein's formula for special relativity: $E=mc^2$. This deceptively simple formula sparked questions: What if we could create an equation to guide the personal and professional brands of our colleagues, clients, and their businesses to relevance? What would the elements of relevance be, and how would they relate to one another?

We have identified four key dynamics of relevance that can be applied to the life of a person, an organization, or a product.

THE FOUR DYNAMICS OF RELEVANCE

The Key

Au = Authenticity

M = Mastery

E = Empathy

Ac = Action

R = Relevance

The Formula

$$(Au + M^2 + E) \times (Ac) = R$$

AUTHENTICITY

Relevance begins with the journey inward to understand the individual authentic self. The maxim "know thyself" is a timeless aphorism; understanding our strengths and our weaknesses with clarity is as vital to a meaningful life today as it was in the time of the Greek sages. Only by digging deep down to the core of our true self can we come to a place of inner certainty. Our underlying values and priorities are our personal navigational stars on life's journey—essential tools to chart a life course that embraces what matters most to us.

The process of revealing the authentic self can be likened to the task by which the sculptor reveals the sculpture within the stone. Think of the Michelangelo masterpiece *David*. The colossal marble block from the quarries of Carrara languished for 25 years before Michelangelo was awarded the commission to carve what has become one of the most recognized works of sculpture. When asked how he made his statues, Michelangelo is reported to have explained that he had only to hew away the rough stone that imprisoned the David within.

Admittedly, chipping away what is extraneous to our true self is not quite so easy as Michelangelo makes it sound. Laurels are difficult to relinquish, even when they do not reflect our true self and deepest principles. We are vulnerable to the seduction of popular recognition, advanced degrees, and job titles guaranteed to impress. The dazzle of accumulated information makes us sound worldly and accomplished, even as it may mask the work of art within. Perhaps, we tell ourselves, earning one more degree, serving on one more board, or adding one more fascinating factoid to our collection of information will make us feel impressive enough, prestigious enough, relevant enough.

But we cannot defeat the forces of commoditization—or live a relevant life—in an assumed identity. It is tempting, but dangerous, to embrace an inaccurate sense of our own importance. Our real selves are waiting for us. It is only by accepting and embracing the real self that we first begin to have an identity of our own. The journey to the real self requires a form of soulful minimalism with a simple litmus test: Have we become the person our childhood self would revere?

In order to come to wisdom, we need to concentrate less on what we know and have, and more on who we are. It is when we chisel away the distractions and compulsive trappings that we come face to face with our authentic self. The key to being authentic is to know ourselves and understand our natural skills, and to map that unique inner self to our outer self. Are the gifts that are within us being translated to the gifts that we are bringing to others? Like our DNA, our unique self can create a unique relevance that is the ultimate vaccine against becoming a commodity. Too many of us are pretty good at what we do for a living, but we aren't tapping our core gifts in our work. Authenticity isn't about being pretty good. It's about excellence in the development of our unique gifts.

MASTERY

In our formula for relevance, we've found that the movement from authenticity to mastery to empathy to action is most successful when it happens sequentially. We can't skip around, developing signature strengths first, then putting them into action and contemplating authenticity sometime later. It's not possible to dedicate ourselves to mastering our signature strengths until we know—by exploring our authentic core—what those signature strengths are. Have we identified our signature strengths and figured out what we are here to do? Once we have, the next step is to develop mastery of them.

It is wonderful to have a natural aptitude for speed or persuasion or musical composition, but aptitude isn't enough. The natural runner who never conditions her body or builds her endurance won't win a marathon by relying on raw talent. Charismatic persuasive speakers won't prevail in a courtroom without a thorough understanding of the rules of law and experience with jury dynamics. Without exploring and practicing musical techniques, raw musical talent will not unfold into soul-stirring sound. Gifts, once identified, must be developed; and that requires discipline and dedication.

Mastery means more than merely engaging in the enjoyable aspects of our talents. True mastery requires skill in every aspect of our gifts. If our gift is marketing, it's not enough to spend all of our time on the glamorous aspects of the advertising industry. Tempting as it is to focus on dreaming up creative ideas, delivering spellbinding presentations, and directing evocative photo shoots, there's more to a successful agency than the glitz. Advertising is a business. In order to run it successfully, we have to develop mastery over the mundane necessities: understanding balance sheets, time sheets, income statements, and business projections. If we hope to be relevant, we must understand the big picture in order to excel at what we do.

As someone who loves to be in the woods, Tom deeply admires those who know every plant, insect, and animal, and who understand the vagaries of the terrain. While mastery can't ward off bad weather, it can enable the seasoned woodsman to pitch a tent that will survive weather's onslaught. As you may have noticed, mastery in our equation is squared. The effect of mastery on relevance is exponential. The difference between one and nine is eight, but the difference between one and nine squared is 80. Squaring mastery reflects the power of deliberately well-honed skills to separate us from the pack.

We see the word "mastery" as an expression of greatness. It implies a command of authentic skills and the judgment to anticipate outcomes based on past lessons.

EMPATHY

So we've dug down into our authentic self, and we are practicing mastery of our unique strengths. How do we make the gifts we've developed relevant to others? How do we build relationships, engage with colleagues, and present professional services in a way that matters more to the lives we touch? We think we have to learn to be interested—in our colleagues, our clients, and their customers. Look for common ground, and seek to comprehend others through empathy. Until we fully comprehend that life is not about just us, it is not fully lived. Upping our level of empathy in our personal and business life is perhaps the most difficult task of all, but like the other dynamics, it is essential.

We think of empathy as the docking station of relevance, with a three-step path signified by "them," "you," and "do." The first step is to focus on "them": what does our friend, colleague, or client care about? The second step is about asking "you"—yourself—what you can bring to their concerns. Finally, "do" focuses us on defining the actions we can take to be an additive force to positively affect the concerns of the others within our scope. Focusing on being interested allows us to connect with those who need what we have to offer. It strengthens our empathy muscle, allowing it to be put to powerful use everywhere in our lives. The ability to assume someone else's perspective, to understand their unmet needs, and to define what we can contribute allows us to offer them the right thing at the right time. It enables us to matter more to others—and for others.

All that matters cannot always be measured. Business empathy is becoming increasingly important as the world shifts to a "demand creation" culture. In a global sales environment, empathy is even more essential. How we sell is as important as what we sell. How we occupy our space deeply matters; it is the lone distinguisher in a sea of sameness.

The empathetic business model focuses on elevating a client's value proposition: how do we make the client more valuable to their customers? In order to answer this question, we have to step beyond our client to the customers they serve, understand the customers' needs, and bring that understanding back to our client. When we understand what drives our client's success, we have a deeper insight into the value proposition they rely on, and we can work with them to elevate their value proposition to better reflect and respond to their customers' concerns.

ACTION

The decision to put authenticity, mastery, and empathy into action is the great differentiator between dreams of potential and the reality of accomplishment. Our talents are finite; the accountant may never write a best-seller, the research scientist may never argue before the Supreme Court, and the surgeon may never win an Oscar. Yet, the decision to put our talents into action is ours to seize. Our formula adds the first three dynamics together and then multiplies their sum by action. Relevance requires authentic skills executed with mastery and reflecting an empathetic understanding of others. We can plug in generous numbers for authenticity, mastery, and empathy, but no matter how large a sum we get, if we multiply it by zero action, we get zero. Only action can move us from necessary preparation to actualizing relevance in our lives.

Just as authenticity has its challenges, so too does the decision to act. A plethora of choices makes us feel that the world is our oyster. Deciding on one option means closing doors to other options—we can be reluctant to commit to a single path when we know it means forgoing others. We can acquire a detailed road map for the life journey we envision, and the most stunningly engineered sports car in the country, but unless we fill the tank with gas, slide behind the wheel, turn the key, and set out on the open road, our careful maps and prize vehicle will take us exactly nowhere.

We have developed tools to help with the decision-making process, and we've identified guidelines to maximize the impact of our actions.

RELEVANCE

Do we matter? Or are we a mere commodity, interchangeable with other people, chosen for the sole reason that we are cheaper than everyone else? When we are relevant, we matter in this world—we are needed. And the more relevant we are, the more we can make choices about what we do, where we do it, and how much we can charge for the services we provide. This is our goal: to be more relevant in our lives and in our work.

Relevance requires us to become "loyal to the logic" of change. In order to initiate any change in our life, whether it is the decision to read this book or drop a few pounds or stop smoking, we have to be convinced that the benefits of change outweigh the cost of inaction. We aren't motivated to change until there's something in it for us. We won't change our thought process or lose weight or stop smoking until our self-interest is served. Unless we see a benefit in mattering, we'll never matter more.

WHERE DO WE GO FROM HERE?

So, how do we do it, you ask. How do we become relevant to our clients, to our market, and to one another? How do we move toward mattering more?

Guidelines and formulas—even good ones—can't change our lives overnight. In the pages to come, we'll identify tools that can be used, as well as the rewards to be discovered when we cultivate relevance in our lives and in our careers. We invite you to step onto the path to relevance and join us on the journey to mattering more.

Our journey begins not by searching for some lofty peak, but by looking within ourselves to discover the unique gifts that are essential to matter more.

AUTHENTICITY

$$(\mathbf{A_u} + M^2 + E) \times (A_c) = R$$

WHAT MAKES YOU SO SPECIAL?

This is where relevance begins. Without authenticity, we are only a poor imitation of someone else. The key to being authentic is to map our inner self to our outer self. Consider: are the gifts that are within us being translated to the gifts that we are bringing to others? Like our DNA, our unique self can create a unique relevance that is the ultimate vaccine against becoming a commodity. Without first understanding our authentic self, the next steps on the journey to relevance will be impossible.

We came of age without any expectation of an above-average birthright. Our own childhoods were decidedly average. We dutifully completed our homework. We learned our lessons and read the books assigned by our teachers. Our clarity of recall during the march through education humbly leaves much to be desired. Yet, as we look back now, we can see, here and there, glimmers of our core selves resonating with the ideas that would come to shape our lives. While poring over literature, history, and science, the authentic self quietly claimed its inspiration and tucked it away until later, when the time was right.

Like seeds planted and nurtured with care, some influences take root swiftly: you may glimpse the musician in the child who sits happily at the piano for hours, the physician in the youngster who tends a menagerie of injured animals, or the writer in the child scribbling away in notebooks. These are gifts that could be called "window moments," glimpses of a passion in progress. In these moments, we experience a union of what we are and what we seek. Other experiences may beglamour us in the moment, but don't find permanent purchase in our core selves.

Some seeds take root, but do not come to fruition for decades. As we reflect on our own experiences with identifying the authentic self, we find that authenticity is a continual process of building self-awareness, a journey through which we acknowledge both our strengths and our limitations, and come to identify a noble purpose. Winston Churchill's noble purpose was to save his "island race." Harper Lee put pen to paper to illuminate the racism she had witnessed in her Alabama hometown. Lincoln was determined to preserve the Union. Susan B. Anthony assumed the mantle of advocate for women's rights.

Our own authentic strengths might not spur us to quite such historically lofty goals as Churchill, Lee, Lincoln, and Anthony, but each of us has unique talents that resonate with the core of who we are. With honesty and a little digging, we have the opportunity to identify our gifts and harness them in the service of our best self—our own unique noble purpose.

BECOMING A GREEK GEEK.

For us, nothing has been as instructive in exploring the notion of authenticity as relearning the work of the great philosophers Aristotle and Plato. We are struck by their applicability to our work as we help companies and people develop their brands.

Why do these early philosophers have so much to say that is helpful to modern marketers? We believe it is because they were focused on the fundamental issues of authenticity that we all face: Who are we? Why are we? How should we behave? Asking these questions encourages us to deepen our self-awareness. In particular, this issue of "who are we?" is critical. Knowing who we are is the key to elevating our capacities and performance.

The dynamics of relevance are the same for brands as they are for people. Being relevant requires authenticity, mastery, empathy, and action. Too many companies—and individuals—are befuddled by delusion when it comes to identifying their authentic strengths and projecting those strengths through their brand. It's as if they live in Opposite Land. If their service is wretched, they tell people that they are great at service. If they are selling a mediocre car, they expound on its hip sportiness. Claiming that you are what you are not will obscure the strengths you do have while destroying your credibility. It's a lose-lose proposition. In order to hunt down and accurately tag authenticity, we must first pop the balloon of self-delusion. It is a painful task. Fortunately, Plato makes it less painful.

SPELUNKING FOR TRUTH.

Plato gave the notion of reality a great deal of thought. He developed an allegory to help people understand how their perceptions distort reality. It's called the Allegory of the Cave. He asks us to imagine a group of people who have been chained in a cave all their lives. Their line of sight is limited to a blank wall, and they spend their days watching shadows of objects cast onto this wall. They come to believe that the shadows don't merely represent the objects— they actually are the objects. The shadows become their reality.

One day, one of them escapes from the chains and makes his way out of the cave and into the world. He sees an object—a tree—and realizes that what he'd thought of as a tree was only a flickering shadow and not a tree at all. He grasps the distinction between perception and reality: the first philosopher is born. He goes back into the cave to share his understanding, encouraging his group to look beyond the shadows and identify the real.

We believe that it is the job of each of us to step outside of ourselves, look beyond the shadows, and seek reality. If we hope to present an authentic self to the world, it is critical that we understand what is real and true about ourselves. So how do we begin to see our companies, our brands, our products, or ourselves as we really are? For us, the best way to start is to stop watching shadows and start facing reality.

NOTHING LIMITS YOU LIKE
NOT KNOWING YOUR LIMITATIONS.

Balancing a bank account is drudgery. Like all drudgery, we put it off as long as possible. When we are fearful of what we will find when we assess our funds, we postpone the task even longer. During these times, we soothe our minds by dwelling on the deposits we've made—while having only vague notions of the amounts of our withdrawals.

The same dynamic comes into play when we endeavor to take an inventory of our lives. We spend most of our time focusing on our assets. Our deficits barely rate a passing glance. But this is not the path to an authentic assessment. Reality requires that we be fearless and take the time to understand our limitations as deeply as we understand our strengths. In a world eager to believe that all of us are above average, and where gold stars are handed out for breathing, we are in danger of believing we can do anything. But we cannot. True authenticity is tethered to reality. A sailor may boast that there are no weather conditions he cannot master, without having sailed in treacherous winds. A tenacious saleswoman may seek a prestigious promotion to a managerial position, but without the leadership strengths to motivate her sales force. A cellphone company may develop cutting-edge technology, but bring it to market without the service resources to provide a positive customer support experience.

Many talents may look desirable as we navigate the possibilities we encounter along life's journey. However, the only talents we can honestly claim are those that are rooted in our authentic core. Embracing the gifts that resonate in our nature is a cornerstone of relevance and one of the most effective ways to beat back commoditization. When we are committed to authenticity, we list on our personal inventories only those skills that have the ease of core familiarity. Other skills may be enviable and desirable, even as we recognize that they will never feel natural to us. A talent that flows through the core of one person will be beyond the grasp of someone else. Using authenticity to identify the skills we choose to master is not only a recipe for success; it is also a recipe for avoiding disaster.

Attempting to claim skills that are not rooted in our core can take us to the point of exhaustion in our lives. Authenticity helps us to evaluate our strengths and understand our value. When we seek excellence within our capabilities, there is an increased probability that we will be rewarded with satisfaction. When we try to force expectations that are beyond our capabilities, we are more likely to experience frustration, discouragement, and mediocrity. We get further when we navigate by our core strengths than we do by trying to claim success through skills for which we feel no passionate resonance or natural aptitude.

Not knowing our limitations is dangerous. Our sailor may have spent his life on the water, but he would be putting himself—and his passengers—in danger if he took a boat out on Lake Superior without regard for ominous weather conditions. By accepting a promotion requiring a skill set she does not possess, our star saleswoman could jeopardize her company's bottom line and her own career. A new product rollout without appropriate customer service support might spell disaster for genuinely innovative technology.

Most truth is hiding in plain sight. We often don't see it, given our myopia of self-interest. Accepting the truth about our limitations matters as much as identifying our strengths. An accurate self-image is more important than a good self-image. If our image is accurate, and we don't like it, we can always do something about it.

THE DANGERS OF DISTRACTION.

Distraction leaches the authenticity out of our communications. When we are not emotionally present, we are gliding over the surface of our interactions and we never tangle in the depths where the nuances of our skills are tested and refined. A medical professor describes the easy familiarity with which her digital-native resident students master medical electronic records—but is troubled by the fact that they enter data with their eyes focused on their digital devices, not on the patient in the room with them. Preoccupation with technology acts as a screen between the student and the patient's real emotion, real fear, and real concern. It may also prevent these residents from noticing physical symptoms that the patient fails to mention. The easy busyness of medical record entry is a way to sidestep the more challenging dynamics of human connection. But experienced physicians know that interpersonal skills are essential to mastering the art and science of medical diagnosis.

People are hungry to interact with those who respond attentively. We love technology as much as the next person, but we realize that when we are interacting with a digital device, we aren't present in the present. If we sit over drinks or dinner engaged by our iPhone instead of with our companions, we squander the opportunity for valuable connection and the benefit of personal accountability that is necessary for growth. If we avoid conflict by using technology, texting, and email as an emotional shield, we lose the opportunity for growth that comes with facing and resolving problems. A fully engaged life requires interaction and connection, not avoidance and electronic isolation.

USE SCALES INSTEAD OF MIRRORS.

It is natural for all of us to seek out sources of information that are most likely to give us feedback with a positive slant. But trusting our self-perceptions alone is a reckless way to gain a grip on reality. Even the most honest person on the planet is an expert at lying to himself or herself.

Looking inward with honesty is not an easy task. It takes time and reflection to evaluate our life experiences, strip away what is extraneous, and come to our core. Is there a talent we have employed, in various forms, throughout our career? Sometimes this can be a clue to a core skill. Another technique is to consult others who know us and whose insights we respect. Those who know us best can sometimes help us recognize gifts when we are unaware of them. They can also help us to distinguish between our genuine gifts and the seductive gifts we don't have, but wish we could claim. Additionally, it may be instructive to pay attention to the things we do easily and with pleasure—the tasks that feel natural and instinctive to us. We might discover signature strengths in the skills we bring to these tasks. Identifying and understanding our natural strengths will give us the best clues about our gifts and our purpose.

If authenticity is the goal, we have to find ways to look at ourselves from the outside in. In marketing, we are loyal to reality by doing research and product testing, and by comparing ourselves to our competition. In our professional and our personal lives, we surround ourselves with respected advisers who will tell us the truth—even when the truth is painful—instead of telling us what we want to hear.

PUT YOUR BEST FOOT FORWARD, BUT MAKE SURE IT'S ATTACHED TO YOUR LEG.

Venturing beyond Plato's cave to achieve a realistic understanding of our capabilities and limitations takes dedication and honesty. With a sane estimate of our authentic strengths in hand, it's our task to present ourselves to the world while circumventing two potential pitfalls:

- **An authentic voice has the pragmatism to rein in aspirations that might otherwise outpace what we can realistically deliver.**

- **An authentic voice has the courage to step away from deniability and embrace accountability.**

We all aspire to be the best. But when our longing to realize our "above average" destiny isn't supported by the nuts-and-bolts rankings, dreams of greatness may tempt us to overstate our gifts. Car rental company Avis had the good sense to resist that temptation. Avis admitted that their competitor, Hertz, was the market leader. Instead of charging into an uphill battle with Hertz to try to capture the number-one spot, Avis embraced its second-place standing with a slogan that was meaningful, memorable, and authentic: "We Try Harder." Then they spent a year training their people to try harder. When they felt confident that their message was tethered to their reality, they launched the Try Harder campaign. Consumers responded positively to the authenticity of their mission to work harder to please.

THERE'S NOT MUCH PROMISE IN UNDERPROMISING.

On the flip side of overpromising is the safety of underpromising, an equally dangerous strategy that causes companies to sink to the lowest common denominator. When we play it safe, we sabotage our chance to make our mark in a memorable, authentic way. Health care organizations confront pressures to provide more responsive, personal care with cost efficiency, striving to provide the industry's "patient-centered care" goal. However, when every hospital system and specialty clinic cautiously claims to provide "patient-centered care"—because all of their competitors claim to provide "patient-centered care"—their claim becomes so safe that they disappear into the din of their competitors' identical claims.

THE MEAN IS ALSO NOT VERY NICE.

When companies succumb to the commoditization of the mean, they trade the joy of distinction for the safety of conformity. The pressures to hunker at the lowest common denominator can include:

- **Concern about the perception of others.** Before law firms relaxed the codes governing self-promotion, every lawyer's letter was written on black and white engraved stationery. There was safety in the indistinguishability of one firm's correspondence from another's—and no authenticity. When we shackle our behavior to the mean, we function in a prison cell of concern about the perception of others. Our choices are safe, but such safety trades uniqueness for conformity, and authenticity for a commoditized identity.

- **Nonaccountability.** When we make ourselves accountable, others are going to be watching to see whether we hit the mark. The pressure is on. Not every company, or individual, thrives on expectant scrutiny. Some are tempted to avoid the scrutiny by loitering through life. These people avoid disappointing others by being disappointing.

- **Fatigue and frustration.** Unlike Sisyphus, the doomed Greek, we aren't cursed for eternity with a big rock that we can't quite push to the summit. However, when our innovative work isn't recognized or rewarded, eventually most of us will stop being innovative. The frustration of getting nowhere wears us down, and we simply stop striving. Instead of actively exploring alternate paths to fulfillment, we opt to do what we need to do, and no more. We quit trying and stay put.

When we gather around the mean without the motivation to try for an authentic best, our performance suffers, and fulfillment drifts out of reach. We have developed an approach to reactivate interest in authentic performance and re-energize motivation. It works for individuals as well as organizations. We use three steps to move away from the mean and toward authenticity:

- **Develop a clear vision of the future.**

- **Provide positive urgency with a compelling reason to act.**

- **Create a personalized connection between desired change and self-interest.**

TRUE TO SELF; REAL TO OTHERS.

Each of us is a unique combination of malleable strengths and limitations. In a world of increasing complexity, we are constantly challenged to upgrade our human operating system by continually compensating for our limitations and honing our strengths. We have come to think of our authentic core as a self-directed, transitional work in progress, rather than a fixed, unchanging destination. We don't "arrive" at authenticity. We reconfirm our evolving fidelity to core self through every chapter of life's journey.

We are motivated to change when we find our own personal and self-interested reasons to become loyal to a new way of thinking. No one wants to be told what to do; not our clients, our spouses, our colleagues, or our children. In fact, we so resist being told what to do that when we are ordered to take action, we feel a powerful compulsion to do the exact opposite—even if we might have had genuine interest in the action we are ordered to take.

Ordering people to change is ineffective, and we are skeptical of anyone who claims to have a foolproof program to change lackluster employees into an ace team. It is far more effective—and exciting—to acknowledge the fallibility of orders up front. We create incentives for real change by personalizing the benefits for us if we change. By exploring the benefits we will reap if we change, and recognizing how change outweighs the cost of inaction, we close the loop of "what's in it for us." This is the space where change becomes possible.

How we present ourselves at any given time is dependent on the situation. We constantly balance the tension of high aspirations with the pragmatism of realistic expectations. The key is to represent ourselves in such a way that we can fulfill the expectations we create. To go back to the bank balance analogy—we don't make withdrawals that our bank account can't cover. The brand promise—for a company and for an individual—lives somewhere between who we are and who we want to be, just as long as who we want to be is tethered to reality.

The example Tom likes to give is this: If he tells people that he looks like a young George Clooney, disappointment is bound to ensue when he appears. If, however, he tells them that he looks like a middle-aged Peter Boyle (think *Young Frankenstein* or *Everybody Loves Raymond*), they can find him in a crowded restaurant in a minute. Take a look at Tom's photo: young George Clooney or middle-aged Peter Boyle?

AUTHENTICITY STARTS WITH REALITY.

Attaining relevance without authenticity is nearly impossible, and attaining authenticity without understanding reality is completely impossible. Authenticity is the outward expression of our inner reality. To ignore reality and choose an inauthentic life or career is the fastest route to becoming commoditized.

Reflection is the key to unlocking self-awareness, and self-awareness in turn opens the doorways to authenticity, character, and purpose. Knowing who we are is the key to elevating our capacities and performance. It is our distinct authentic self, standing apart from the low roar of commoditized individuals and organizations, that establishes unique value.

The journey of authenticity is an evolving one. Childhood passions may nudge us along a series of steppingstones—or through a maze of snake arms—that lead us into a satisfying career path. We will certainly express our core selves in different ways at different stages of our lives. Our self-awareness at 18 will probably be markedly different from our expression of self-realization at 55. The guidance of our inner reality slowly and surely develops into the outward expression of our authentic brand—as both individuals and organizations.

THE THREE HALVES.

We see the authentic path of relevance undergoing three shifts over the course of a person's life, through what we think of as "the three halves of life":

- **Hard work.** This is the work we do in the first part of our life to identify and develop the skills that resonate at our authentic core. Think of it as building the professional container to hold your goals and objectives. Here we develop the mastery that enables us to matter more in the world. We are learning who we are and who we are not; what we are good at and what we are not.

- **Right work.** As our skills develop, we begin to focus on the goals and objectives we're determined to achieve. If life's dual bottom line measures both our net worth and our life worth, this is the stage of life where we build our net worth with our life worth in mind, and invest in our personal equity. Right work is characterized by the development of significance and substance.

• **Life work.** The third half of life is about releasing our accumulated gifts into the world. After creating and filling our container comes the time when we share our wealth for the benefit of others. The career of Bill Gates exemplifies a life lived in three halves. Gates spent the early part of his life mastering computer technology and then used his skills to build the container that is Microsoft. Now Gates is using the fruits of his success to establish the Bill and Melinda Gates Foundation, which funds more than two dozen global initiatives in health, development, and education.

Most of our clients are living and focused in the middle stage—on the right work of the second half of life. But our perception of the demographic in that middle stage is shifting. Ask for a definition of middle age, and you are likely to get a laugh and a quip that 60 is the new 40. Under the laughter, what we are sensing in both business and society are people in their late 40s and 50s who are deeply concerned about slipping into irrelevance. Younger professionals harbor parallel concerns about the relevance of skill sets that are constantly under pressure to keep pace with technology and shifts in the global market. Once, we might have defined the boundary between our first and second halves of life with a number. "When you turn 30, you move from building your career container to filling that container with achievements," we might have said. But the marker has moved.

AN EVENT TO REMEMBER.

How do we define the transitional bridge from the first half of life to the second in today's world? We no longer consider a 30th birthday the symbolic rite of passage into the second "right work" stage of life. Today, we view this bridge as an event, or a series of events, challenging us to reflect on and recommit to our core values. The bridge may be a mentor who guides us to a new tier of performance and business acumen. It may be an inspired moment that connects us viscerally to our passion. Another accelerator of authenticity is adversity.

In life, patterns repeat themselves until we address them. To get our attention, life can throw us a pebble in the form of a career roadblock that forces us to reassess our priorities. If that doesn't work, a stone, and if that doesn't get our attention, a brick. We refer to the bricks of life as The Great Humblings—crises that overwhelm us. A Humbling might be a health emergency, a relational or financial breakdown, or some other critical loss.

Many events can herald the transition from the first half to the second half; it is a transition that has little or nothing to do with age. One 20-something salesperson transitioned from first to second half through the experience of battling cancer. Shaken to the core by the indignities of this terrible disease at a young age, this individual developed what we term second-half wisdom. For others, the authentic self lies fallow during a career blanketed in the illusion of security. It may take a sudden job loss in midlife to prompt us to dig deep into an inventory of our values and dreams, and emerge on a new career path entirely—one that embraces our authentic values in a way that our first career did not.

In terms of significance, the nature of the transitional experience doesn't matter so much as our response to it does. These transitional events tend to elicit a set of responses—some deeply affirming and transformative, and others less helpful. We want to explore the way these responses can shape our determination to travel our path with authenticity.

VALENTINE'S DAY 1886: THE DAY CHISELED IN SOUTH DAKOTA GRANITE.

When Tom first saw Mount Rushmore in person on a family vacation, there seemed something odd about it. He looked up at those magnificent visages, a bit perplexed. His mind ran through the great presidents in our country's history: George Washington, check; Thomas Jefferson, check; Abraham Lincoln, check; Theodore Roosevelt, huh? What was Teddy doing up there? And how is it that the man who would lend his name to a stuffed bear should be placed after Jefferson and before Lincoln? It made no sense to Tom, either in chronology or importance. But now, he was curious.

For many, Teddy is the other Roosevelt who was president. He didn't take us out of the Great Depression or defeat the Nazis. We may remember his big stick and how he was a sickly child who became a cowboy, but not much more than that. So why was it that just eight years after his death and 18 years after the end of his presidency, he was viewed as a peer of the greatest presidents in our history? How did he become the one post-Civil War president who really mattered? We believe that Teddy's place on the South Dakota monument is the result of a single day, 16 years before he became president.

The giants immortalized on Rushmore are recognized for leading our nation with determination and the courage to follow their convictions. Their heroic responses in times of national crisis are documented across the pages of history. But before these men rose to confront the challenges of nations, they were faced with other crises—some of a quiet and deeply personal nature. We believe that these private trials, and the path that leaders like Roosevelt charted in response, set them on the road to greatness.

For Teddy Roosevelt, challenge appeared in catastrophic form. But choosing an authentic life does not always require a brick of life-shattering proportions. A brick's worth of challenge in one life may be a stone along another traveler's journey and a pebble on a third person's path. Others may not find authenticity through challenge at all, but through the encouragement of a mentor or teacher. Regardless of the source—crisis or teacher—mastering the lessons of authenticity is critical to charting the course of a relevant life.

Teddy Roosevelt seemed destined for a life of fortunate ease. He was born into wealth. His father was generous and civic-minded. His stunning Southern belle mother was rumored to have been the inspiration for *Gone with the Wind*'s Scarlett O'Hara. Teddy was the apple of her eye. He gazed out at the world from the cosseted pinnacle of New York society. A sickly child, he became a great reader and writer on all things natural.

Through his early 20s, Teddy led a charmed life. When he was smitten with Alice Hathaway Lee at their first meeting, he enlisted the help of his popular mother to win the hand of the striking blonde with a cheerful disposition that earned her the nickname "Sunshine." After courting her with single-minded determination for more than a year, the enraptured Roosevelt announced their engagement on February 14. His professional life flourished with equal success. One year after graduating from Harvard, he was elected to the New York State Legislature. On February 12, 1884, Roosevelt was attending to Assembly business when he learned that his wife had given birth to a healthy baby girl. In that moment, Roosevelt was on top of the world. Fortune was smiling on his professional aspirations and bestowing the happiest of blessings on his personal life. The future was golden, and joyful beyond what he had imagined.

Two days later, joy came to an abrupt end.

Eager to hold his new daughter, Roosevelt left the Assembly for his ancestral home, arriving on his anniversary, February 14. He was stricken to find his wife semicomatose due to complications of pregnancy, and his mother gravely ill with typhoid. He held his wife for hours, willing her back to health, and leaving her only briefly to be with his fading mother. Despite his desperate efforts and the best of medical resources, both women died that day, within hours of each other. The depth of Roosevelt's grief was staggering. He marked a black "X" through February 14 on his calendar. His diary entry for that terrible day was a single stark sentence: "The light has gone out of my life." He would never write or speak of this loss again.

THE BEGINNING OF TRUE GREATNESS.

That devastating February 14 was, for Teddy Roosevelt, a Great Humbling, the large-brick lesson that forces us to come to terms with who we are. We believe that without this day, Roosevelt would be a footnote in history instead of the heroic figure monumentalized on Mount Rushmore. Occasions of terrible loss

bring us to our knees—but they also present an opportunity, if we choose it, to reach to our core and reaffirm our authentic self.

Those of us who have faced a Humbling know that difficult circumstances can cause us to question our values. When an economic downturn sends us into the street with our prestigious title stripped away and our career path derailed, there is no option but to make choices. We may find strength we didn't know we had to pursue our goals with more tenacity than before, or find ourselves waylaid by insecurities and fears that we were able to gloss over while the road was smooth and level. Disappointments test our strengths and lay bare our weaknesses. Sometimes the losses stagger us, other times they are merely bothersome. Large or small, our response to setback reveals our core values and the principles that are bedrock to our personal authenticity.

More important, our reaction to disappointment starts to build the habits that gradually establish our operating system. As Roosevelt observed: "Nothing in the world is worth having or worth doing unless it means effort, pain, difficulty. ... I have never in my life envied a human being who led an easy life; I have envied a great many people who led difficult lives and led them well." If a Great Humbling arrives at our door, some of us, like Teddy Roosevelt, will find the courage to follow the path of our authentic selves. Others will be less fortunate.

It is one thing to imagine how we might respond to a crisis; it is quite another to face a personal disappointment. Imagined courage does not always withstand the onslaught of reality. We can't really know how we will react until we find ourself in the thick of a challenge—and many of us are taken by surprise.

A Great Humbling is not a run-of-the-mill disappointment. It won't be shrugged off, and it doesn't respond to a positive affirmation. This is an event that unsettles our confidence and shakes us to our core. Anyone who has faced a devastating loss will resonate with Roosevelt's experience. They know the feeling—as though the floor has suddenly given way in the face of a loss that cannot be fixed. In the throes of a Great Humbling, it is a struggle to wrap the mind around the circumstances that have befallen. Sometimes the best we can

do is to follow the advice attributed to the other great Roosevelt: "When you're at the end of your rope, tie a knot and hold on." The enormity of the crisis leaves us no choice but to literally get real.

As we have explored our ideas about the nature of authenticity with clients, colleagues, and friends, they react powerfully to the concept of The Great Humbling and to the notion that there is value in challenge, even when the challenge is unwelcome. Many recognize their own experiences in the stories we relate. A cancer diagnosis, the failure of a business built on a life's dream, a physical injury, the death of a beloved family member or friend, a financial loss, the dissolution of a marriage, a bout with depression—all of these painful events can trigger self-reflection.

Individual journeys unfold along a parallel storyline: a loss or a challenge serves as a catalyst for self-reflection and a regrouping into a stronger, more authentic life. The journey may be short or long, merely inconvenient or deeply painful. For those of us who navigate it successfully, it is an invaluable lesson that reconnects us with the values at our core, and with the authentic self we aspire to be.

In the case of Great Humbling experiences, people repeatedly described a sense of being utterly alone. We recognize the chord of truth in this observation. In our day-to-day lives, we don't always acknowledge the realities of dark journeys. The temptation is to gloss over the sense of shame, or mask loss with glib positive affirmations—as though a self-help mantra could have filled Roosevelt's emptiness as he buried both his wife and his mother.

Any of us is susceptible to crisis, but, as others have discovered, things are rarely as helpless as they look. The road back from significant loss may not be easy or painless, and not everyone emerges unscathed. Yet we have seen these experiences serve a critical purpose for determined individuals: you can choose to carve a path out of difficulty to a richer, more authentic life.

We aren't going to give you a flip line about how you can control your own universe. We don't believe that. It's a mess out there, and it's going to get messier. In the complex and unpredictable global community that is our world today,

we are afloat on a sea of insecurity. We can't change the sea. But we do believe that we can create islands on that sea—islands of stability in a permanently unstable world. A Great Humbling, or a lesser crisis, can force us to identify sources of personal strength that will stand firm against life's storms. Roosevelt defined courage not as having the strength to go on, but as going on even when we don't have the strength. We believe that an affirming course can be charted through the storm. Life's challenges can be survived. They can also transform a life with a clarion call to authenticity.

THE PATH TO RUSHMORE.

Teddy Roosevelt always had amazing gifts. But his early life did not force him to hone them. He was like a seedling covered with a thick blanket of leaves. It was The Great Humbling that swept the leaves away, allowing his authentic self to flourish. Through the choices Roosevelt made in coming to terms with his loss, he became the Teddy Roosevelt he was meant be. Anguish stripped him of affectations and revealed his true self. What were passions became actions. What were interests became expertise. He exchanged posturing for purpose. The inner gifts of his early years found full and complete outer expression when Teddy emerged from the crucible of profound grief.

Before The Great Humbling, Teddy was an intellectual, high-society player with a passion for nature and military history. His physical endeavors were limited to organized sports or events like boxing, crew, and hunting expeditions. After the Humbling, Teddy recharted his life, and the journey transformed him into the embodiment of rugged American virtue. He became a cowboy, deputy sheriff, military hero, builder of the Panama Canal, Amazon explorer, Nobel Peace Prize winner, and, to this day, the youngest person to become president of the United States.

THREE ROADS, BUT ONLY ONE LEADS TO RELEVANCE.

Roosevelt charted a course along the narrow, reaffirming road back from loss—the journey that finds, embraces, and nurtures authenticity. This is the path we value. It is not always an easy path to stick to. Along the way, we may stumble or veer off on a tempting but dangerous side road or two. Roosevelt did—but he was able, eventually, to correct his course. Not everyone does.

- **The side road of hubris.** At first, Roosevelt responded to his loss with a futile attempt to deny his experience and its lessons. After laying his mother and wife to rest, he numbly continued with his life along the course that he had set. As if on autopilot, he went forward with plans to build the home at Oyster Bay that he'd promised to his wife. He served as minority leader of the New York State Legislature and chair of a commission that would make major changes to the charter of the City of New York.

Hubris tempts us to take the easy way back from loss. We try to march on as though nothing has changed, wielding hubris like a shield against awareness and self-reflection. We see hubris in the individuals who take no responsibility for the dissolution of a marriage; the executives who lose their position and refuse to acknowledge that the landscape of their profession is irrevocably changing; the dreamers leveled by bankruptcy only to return to the spending behaviors that initially put them at risk. The crisis passes, and we follow pride back to our old patterns of behavior. "Oh man," we think to ourselves. "I don't know what that was, but I'm sure glad it's over." The path of hubris offers no growth and no new awareness. It lures us to continue to put our faith in an impressive-sounding but obsolete title, or in skills that are no longer adequate to the marketplace, or in behaviors with a track record of failure, while waiting for the world to return to the familiar patterns of the past.

Hubris blinds us to the truth that there is no going back. If we are unwilling to take responsibility for our circumstances, we may be tempted to channel our energies into resentment against the world, or against the individuals we blame for our plight. Resentment may appear to be a self-interested strategy, but it is akin to drinking poison and then waiting for your enemy to suffer its effects. Those who continue on the path of hubris remain deliberately unaware that all around them, the world has changed—permanently. The price they pay for their pride is a self-penalizing life.

Roosevelt followed the siren song of hubris for months, but by the time he went as a delegate to the Republican National Convention in June of 1884, he admitted to himself that his life was no longer working. His circumstances had changed, and his old world was gone. He had to find his way to a new life.

• **The side road of helplessness.** When Roosevelt dropped the shield of hubris, he was forced to confront the depths of his loss. Facing the facts of loss is no easy task. Unnerved and feeling unequal to the task of enduring through life's challenges, we can feel crushed by our circumstances. Roosevelt experienced this sense of being unmoored. When he left the East Coast, disillusioned, he claimed that he had no further aspiration but to retire to his ranch in the Badlands of the Dakota Territory.

When our confidence is shattered, it is tempting to slip away into a life of damaged meekness, closing our own aperture of opportunity and choosing a self-limiting life. We can be haunted by thoughts that we are not viable, not relevant, not worthy of happiness. If we allow meekness to become chronic, we may take shelter in mediocrity and never again find the courage to reach out to life's promise. Acting small does not serve our capacity for happiness, and it cripples the potential gifts we might otherwise develop to serve ourselves and the world.

When Roosevelt reached the Badlands of Medora, North Dakota, he built a second ranch along the banks of the Little Missouri River. Resisting self-pity was a matter of survival in the lawless West. Roosevelt threw off helplessness to hunt down horse thieves and outlaws. When he captured three riverboat thieves, he personally escorted them on a 40-hour journey to trial, reading Tolstoy to keep himself awake. In a land in which most high-society swells wouldn't last a week, Roosevelt thrived. He was no longer reading about high adventure, he was living it. Ranching, capturing outlaws, and fighting the elements were balanced with intense study of any topic that captured his wide-flung curiosity.

• **The narrow path to relevance.** Roosevelt may have stumbled along his way, as we humans tend to do, but he was always able to find his way back to the narrow path that nurtures authenticity. He embraced the lesson of humility offered by The Great Humbling, and he married his understanding of fallibility to confidence and pragmatic clarity. He sidestepped the danger of confusing humility with humiliation, reconnected to his core childhood passions for nature and adventure, and used the lessons of The Great Humbling to create greater significance in his life going forward.

Would a Teddy Roosevelt untouched by tragedy have had such an enormous impact on the first half of the 20th century? We cannot know. We do know that Teddy Roosevelt went on to be the most relevant person of his age. In his journey through his Great Humbling, he transformed his life and, in turn, transformed a nation.

Adversity challenges us to dig down to our core, hone our self-understanding, and discard the trappings that don't contribute to an authentic life. We don't arrive at authenticity and move on to something else. It is a direction, not a destination; an ongoing practice that must be exercised daily, because Great Humblings tend not to be one-time events. Many of us will face challenges repeatedly over the course of our lives.

We do believe, however, that a first Humbling or crisis is particularly significant. Our reaction to our first challenge sets the wiring—our response mechanism—for our response to subsequent crises. Behavioral choices establish habits, and habits are strengthened with repetition over time. When we choose the steps to authenticity through our first hurdle, we are putting an authenticity-valuing operating system in place to guide ourselves through future challenges.

What are the steps that can guide us, as they guided Roosevelt, to a reaffirming recovery that reconnects us with our core and enables us to reconstruct our identity in a more authentic way? What tools can help us find the way from helpless bewilderment to courage and the determination to rebuild?

HOW TO SURVIVE A GREAT HUMBLING
IN JUST THREE INCREDIBLY DIFFICULT STEPS.

Tom remembers the advent of his own Great Humbling with rueful clarity. His agency, Riley Hayes, was flourishing. With calm economic seas and brisk business, profitability filled the sails at a speed and volume his agency had never experienced. But the next year, the winds softened to a gentle breeze, enough to keep his agency moving forward, but hardly putting them to the test.

Just as the sails started to go slack, a great opportunity appeared on the horizon. Northwest Airlines, at that time the fifth-largest airline in the country, invited Riley Hayes to pitch for the assignment to develop Northwest's worldwide graphic design system. A win would be a prize account for a big shop, and a massive project for Riley Hayes.

The competition was formidable. The agencies vying for Northwest's work were significantly larger, well known, talented, and influential. But Riley Hayes had something they didn't have: creative director Kerry Krepps, an airline geek who was also a world-class designer. To prepare for the pitch, Riley Hayes pulled Kerry off all her other work and sent her into seclusion in an underground location (her basement). Two weeks later, she emerged with four noteworthy design concepts. Three were outstanding; one was transcendent.

The agencies made their pitches. When the call from Northwest came, Kerry's transcendent concept was chosen, and she and the rest of Tom's staff set about turning her idea into a working document that would define the worldwide graphic standards for every piece of communication the airline produced. Once again the sails were full, the wind was brisk, and Riley Hayes was skimming victoriously out of precarious waters and toward a horizon golden with promise.

With the crisp snap of fall in the air, Riley Hayes was ready to unveil their global branding program to Northwest's worldwide marketing managers and agency partners. Decision makers flew into Minneapolis from all over the world, and the agency threw open the doors of its 100-year-old, yellow brick building overlooking the Mississippi to welcome them. The conference room was packed. The work was a tremendous hit.

Confident of the outcome, Riley Hayes had gone all out to prepare for an evening that would indelibly commemorate success. A decadent catered buffet beckoned guests to partake. The air filled with the strains of a live jazz band. Sparkling cocktails were served with flourish from the full bar. The agency's deck blazed with tiki torches under the clear, star-studded night sky. Toasts were proposed. Champagne corks popped and flutes chimed. The downtown Minneapolis skyline glittered. It was a night cloaked in celebratory perfection.

Tom's agency had navigated not just through financial crisis, but also into the heady realm of national agency greatness. The work for Northwest would grace millions of pieces of communication every year. The agency name would be uttered in sentences with other advertising giants. Tom could almost hear floodgates opening to eager new clients on the rising tides of fortune. As the man with his name on the door, Tom too would gain the recognition he deserved, or maybe more accurately, desired. As he basked in the accolades of his new client and the flickering light of the tiki torches, the night felt magical. He was at the pinnacle of his success on this beautiful evening. He had no way to know that The Great Humbling speeding toward him would also shake our entire nation to its foundations.

The next morning, September 11, 2001, dawned clear and beautiful. Tom had slept in, still enjoying the glow of the previous evening and contemplating the future of abundance that lay before him. The terrible, incomprehensible events that unfolded over the next few hours are firmly fixed in Tom's memory, as they are in the memories of all of us who know exactly where we were when we heard the unimaginable news.

Suffering is never relative. Whatever suffering we undergo, it is virtually impossible for us to measure it against the suffering of others. While others were dying or losing loved ones on that September morning, Tom's business was hurled into crisis. And while Tom recognizes now how trivial his problems were that day in comparison to those of the victims and their families, in the moment, he felt that his world had been destroyed.

Northwest Airlines abruptly stopped flying. They also halted all communications projects, realizing the futility of inviting people to fly with the scenes of smoking towers and crashed planes fresh in their minds. Soon after, Riley Hayes' second-largest client, Marquette Bank, was sold to Wells Fargo. Within 30 days of Riley Hayes' triumphal celebration, the agency lost 70 percent of its revenue.

The succession of disasters brought Tom face to face with the all-encompassing loss that is The Great Humbling. Just as his agency reached the height of success, the national market crumbled, and the fortunes of Tom's agency crumbled with it. Yet, like Roosevelt following the deaths of his wife and mother, Tom found a way to work through his losses and lay the foundation for the significant success his agency enjoys today.

In no way do we mean to imply that tragedy is a good thing. But it has been our experience that tragedies of humbling magnitude can spur a reaction in individuals that sets them on the path to a more authentic life. In making their way back from the Humbling, Roosevelt and Tom, like so many others who have shared their stories with us, dug down to the strength at their core and rebuilt in remarkable ways.

Three steps helped Tom survive his Humbling and move beyond it. Tom would be the first to tell you that it's not that he executed all of them perfectly, but he did follow all of them. As a result, Tom emerged with a deeper sense of who he was and what really mattered to him. The rewards of these survival steps went beyond self-knowledge. Tom took the lessons he learned about himself and incorporated them into the philosophy of his agency. Today, Riley Hayes uses these steps to apply the lessons of authenticity in the service of its clients.

THE FIRST STEP: RESPIRATION.

The most elemental and necessary action we can take in the immediate aftermath of a crisis? Keep breathing. When loss is fresh, it may be all we can do to simply concentrate on the very fundamental act of existence. In fact, in the face of disaster, the determination to continue breathing can be a heroic gesture. Roosevelt may have been moving by rote through his life in the wake of his loss—but he was moving. When Riley Hayes spiraled into deep trouble, Tom focused on one thought: "As long as we are still breathing, we aren't dead."

Tom knew that as bleak as things looked, it was critical to show his staff, his clients, and his industry that he was going to survive and ultimately succeed. Just as breathing keeps a person alive, making payroll keeps a business alive. Tom's agency may not have been more talented or smarter or more experienced than other agencies, but no agency CEO was more motivated than Tom. Every 15 days, Tom made payroll. It was never easy, but Tom knew that he had only one stockholder: himself. If his agency went down, Tom believed there would be no second chance for him.

Tom was completely committed to the survival of Riley Hayes because the survival of his personal life depended on the survival of his agency. Tom's company was not the only one struggling in the aftermath of the 9/11 attacks. Some other agencies had such diffused ownership that failure would not have too dramatic an impact on any one person; for them, the incentive to keep breathing was less acute. Tom believes that the very personal nature of his professional plight motivated him to take the necessary risks that other agencies did not feel driven to take. In a situation that was already precarious, Tom gambled his family's home, taking out a second mortgage—so he could keep making payroll. It was a huge but necessary risk. Because Tom found the determination to do what was necessary to keep breathing, his agency lived to see another day.

THE SECOND STEP: THE RECKONING.

Months went by. It still felt as though the worst had happened, but Tom and his agency continued to breathe. Gradually, Tom realized that although he might not be able to understand why crisis befell him, or tease out the motivations of all of the players in his drama, there was something he could do. He could assess what had happened in terms of his own actions. He could ask the question: "Who am I and where am I now?"

A Great Humbling deconstructs our old world; in the aftermath, that old world is gone for good. We find ourselves at a fork in the road, with a choice to make. One path is a journey of change, a road to deeper authenticity. The other path is an attempt to preserve the status quo by clinging to a self-image from a world that has been swept away. The outcome of authenticity is joy. The outcome of image maintenance is exhaustion. In our work, we have been struck by the number of people who express a sense of exhaustion in their lives. It is our hope to intelligently, confidently, and reflectively explore ways to create a little more lightness in our lives.

The reckoning is a process of acknowledging losses and taking a long hard look in the mirror. As Tom pragmatically evaluated his circumstances, he began to see himself more clearly.

Tom knew that he was not responsible for the terrible things that happened on the morning of 9/11, but he also acknowledged that he was responsible for building a company with a vulnerable foundation. Through years of escalating success, it had been easy to focus on the intriguing creative challenges and leave the nuts and bolts of running a business to someone else. Looking forward, Tom knew that as he rebuilt his agency, there were things he could do better.

Some individuals stumble at this step. Instead of honestly assessing their shortcomings as well as their inner strengths, they succumb to the temptations of hubris or bitterness. It is easier to rail against fate than it is to take a hard look at our own shortcomings. It is less painful to assign blame elsewhere and reassure ourselves that no fault lies with us—that only terrible and undeserved events could have torn our world asunder. Others buckle under the weight of loss, unable to move past defeat. They lose the courage to ever raise their eyes from the ground, reconciling their dreams to defeat.

We are all human. Especially during times of stress, everyone is susceptible to hubris, anger, and feelings of defeat. Reflecting on our pre-crisis self can be like seeing an avatar of ourself that is no longer sustainable. With the avatar stripped away, it is time to have a new conversation with ourself. For some, what is left behind after the Humbling is a burden that slides off with relief, bringing a new sense of freedom and possibility. For others, like Roosevelt, what is lost is not excess; it is what matters very much, on the deepest level. But it's gone, and we simply have to deal with it. Clarity isn't always comforting, but it is honest and authentic, and it is the gift of a Humbling.

Loss doesn't necessarily mean that the life we lived before was an inauthentic one. But it is so easy, when times are good and without significant challenge, to coast into a comfortable rhythm and lose touch with our core. We are all susceptible to the seduction of comfort. We can begin to mistake the rewards earned by our core skills for the core itself. Soon, expecting rewards as our due becomes a habit.

A Humbling shears away rewards and lays bare the flaws of habitual assumptions. There's no choice but to reconnect with our essential skills, our essential self. The Humbling can do for us what Michelangelo did for his masterpiece *David*. It strips away all of the unnecessary stone, all of the trappings, until the essential self is revealed. The reckoning is the part of the journey that compels us to reconnect with the part of our self that can be lost in the hustle of success; the part of our self that makes us who we are; the part that cannot be chiseled away.

For us, one effective reckoning tool is to separate the trappings of image from the qualities that make up our essential nature. Tom, who has always felt at home on the water, likens the process to the principle of the yachtsman's rule. According to this sailor's guideline, when we go out on a voyage, we set aside only the things we need, and then we cut those supplies in half. We strip down to the elemental—the absolutely most essential things. Everything is scrutinized, because everything adds to the burden we carry.

Phil describes this assessment with the carry-on metaphor of road warrior frequent fliers: we don't travel with a fleet of suitcases; we pare down to what will fit in one carry-on. Lighten the load. Cut back to what's utterly essential. Metaphorically, we don't want to check bags.

How do we define what makes the cut? For us, it's an examination. Is a behavior helpful? Is it worth its weight? Do we get more out of it than we put into it? Does it move the ball forward? If the answer is no, then we leave it behind.

What did we find at our core in our own personal journeys? We found some genetic coding. We found some habits, good and bad. We found meaningful relationships and relationships that were no longer useful. Significantly, we honestly identified the things that we were not good at. We came to terms with the qualities we envied but did not possess. We recognized that wanting to be like "that guy," even though we weren't encoded the way "that guy" was, had prompted us to assume avatar selves that had to be discarded.

Today, when Tom is at his best, he evaluates the things in his life based on whether he uses them and whether he finds them essential. Items that don't pass his essential test are jettisoned.

The experience of crisis can reveal the sculpture inside us, as well as the excess stone that accumulates along life's journey. Some of that excess "life rubble" might be unhealthy relationships, debt, self-betrayal, or false imaging. Why did we gather up all that stone in the first place? Looking back, we see reasons. We were compelled by deep insecurity and a need to be valued. In part, we didn't know who we were yet. Is that good or bad? We don't know. We only know that it was true in our lives, and that the time came, through no wisdom on our part, when we could no longer carry unnecessary weight. That stone had to go. We claimed our authenticity when we started stripping away the excess weight that had accumulated in our lives.

THE THIRD STEP: RECONSTRUCTION.

During the reckoning, Tom came to terms with the hard reality that his old formula for success no longer worked. It was time to turn his gaze to the future and pragmatically assess the post-9/11 business climate. He made an inventory of both the strengths he possessed and the errors he had committed. Scanning his list of errors, he asked himself some hard questions. Were his shortcomings caused by a limitation in his skills, or his wisdom, or both? Could he make appropriate corrections himself, or should he turn to others to supplement his skills? In the future, how could his strengths and the supplemental skills he needed be used to create a better, less vulnerable agency?

Once Tom had dug down to take an honest look at himself, he was ready to begin the reconstruction of his life in a more authentic way. He still felt a long way from whole. As he puts it, "It was like a tornado had gone through our home and we were left with a couch, a set of steak knives, a television remote control, and a fully intact game of Twister." It takes more than steak knives and a Twister game to rebuild after a Humbling, but now Tom knew that at least he was alive and had his arms, legs, head, and heart to throw into the task.

Note that we are talking about a task, and the heart and will to rebuild. In our experience, reconstruction cannot be accomplished through visualizations or manifestations to attract the desired outcome—it takes hard work and a lot of it. Aspirations and dreams are important, but Roosevelt did not wish himself from a house in mourning to the presidency. When he found the will to confront the emptiness in his days, his reckoning took him west. There he uncovered and developed the strengths that had lain dormant at his core. He fought, he built, he adventured, he commanded, and he explored. Over years of risk and hard work, he honed the qualities that prepared him for presidential leadership. Roosevelt may have had his eyes on the stars, but he kept his feet on the ground.

One of the strengths that can emerge in periods of reconstruction is an elevated spiritual accuracy about self. There's no energy to drag unnecessary trappings through a period of crisis; these times strip away the extraneous. For many people, the idea of scrapping what no longer matters is a breakthrough thought. Self-help dialogues tend to focus on adding to an aspirational list. There is something freeing about choosing to strip away items instead of assuming more tasks. Clarity of purpose and release of unnecessary burdens can be among the gifts of crisis experiences.

Reconstructing our identity in a more authentic way means going to the core of our self and figuring out what parts of our DNA to retain through challenge, through loss, through change. Which of our skills do we gravitate toward; which of them consistently give us pleasure? Those are the elements we bring to the table as we reconstruct a more stripped-down, authentic self going forward. They are our "insourced" skills. Looking ahead, it's also important to be honest about the skills we require and don't possess. Those are the skills we'll need to "outsource" in order to advance on an evolving playing field.

Tom worked through his own assessment and rebuilding, confronting the dynamic tension between creativity and discipline. He understood the continuing value of his core creative and relational skills, but he also knew he had to push himself beyond that comfort zone. Where in the past he'd had little time for the business of running an agency, now he rolled up his sleeves and plugged away at the financial details. He looked beyond the fading glamour of the splashy print ads and commercials, and analyzed the growing influence of new media as a marketing and relationship-building tool. Recognizing that there were all sorts of emerging marketing tools that could bring his clients success, he had to admit that he knew next to nothing about them. He went about the process of rebuilding his agency with the up-to-date expertise that his clients would need to matter more.

AUTHENTICITY SUMMARY INSIGHTS

Authenticity is the core of relevance. We define authenticity as being true to self and real to others. We believe that it is the job of each of us to step outside of ourselves, look beyond the shadows, and seek what is real and true about ourselves.

Make an unflinching assessment of our limitations. An accurate self-image is more important than a good self-image. If our image is accurate, and we don't like it, we can always do something about it.

Distraction leaches the authenticity out of our communications. When we are not emotionally present, we are not engaged—and we never test or refine the nuances of our skills.

The derailers of authenticity.
- *Concern about the perception of others.*
- *Nonaccountability.*
- *Fatigue and frustration.*

Three steps move us away from the mean and toward authenticity.
- *Development of a clear vision of the future.*
- *Positive urgency with a compelling reason to act.*
- *A connection between desired change and self–interest.*

Our personal brand promise lives somewhere between who we are and who we want to be, as long as who we want to be is tethered to reality.

Authenticity starts with reality. It is impossible to attain authenticity without understanding reality.

The three halves. The authentic path of relevance undergoes three shifts, the "three halves of life," over the course of a lifetime.

- *Hard work. This is the work we do in the first part of our life to identify and develop the skills that resonate at our authentic core.*
- *Right work. As our skills develop, we focus on the goals and objectives we've determined to achieve.*
- *Life work. The third half of life is about releasing our accumulated gifts into the world for the benefit of others.*

The Great Humbling—a crisis that shakes us to our core. A Humbling might be a health emergency, a relational or financial breakdown, or another critical loss. These moments can create our greatest breakthroughs and allow our true self to emerge.

The "narrow road" response to The Great Humbling.

- *The first step: respiration.*
- *The second step: the reckoning.*
- *The third step: reconstruction.*

By knowing our signature strengths and respecting our limitations, we now can nurture those strengths and create a level of mastery that will give us the opportunity to matter more.

MASTERY

$$(A_u + M^2 + E) \times (A_c) = R$$

When it comes to being relevant, being good at what we do isn't good enough. We need to be masterful. Mastery is the ultimate expression of greatness. It implies a command over the elements around us and a foreknowledge of what will happen based on a reverence for the lessons of the past. Mastery is built on authenticity; it informs us about our limits as well as our strengths. In our relevance equation, mastery is squared. The effect of mastery on our relevance is exponential.

If we were to nominate a poster boy whose authenticity embodied the imagination and emotion of the Romantic Movement, the honors would go to Lord George Gordon Byron. Goethe called Byron "the greatest genius of our century." Almost two centuries after his death, Byron is still considered one of the finest poets in the English language.

As a leader of the Romantics, Byron did not merely acknowledge his authentic romantic self, he also developed an unapologetic mastery of every skill a poet is reputed to possess—in both his personal and his literary life. Physically, Byron was the epitome of the dreamy-eyed poet, and he used his dashing looks to maximum effect. He embodied the Byronic hero his writings made famous. His travels through England and across Europe were marked by lavish excess, numerous affairs, and self-imposed exile. The Greeks lauded him as a national hero for his role in the Greek War of Independence.

AN APPLE THAT FELL IN THE NEXT ORCHARD.

As basic biology would dictate, Byron's dalliances resulted in descendants, some known and others mere figments of rumor. Of Byron's verifiable offspring, Augusta Ada King, Countess of Lovelace, possessed gifts that won her a rightful place of her own in history—but in a discipline that could not be further from her father's literary legacy. Born of an educated heiress and the notoriously larger-than-life father she never knew, Ada might have been tempted to set aside her talents for the soft ease of an aristocratic life. Fortunately for the world, that is not the way her story goes.

Ada's life exemplifies the process by which we can choose to identify and then develop our signature strengths with long-term dedication. Like her father, Ada recognized her strengths and actively cultivated them through study, practice, and experience. She honed raw talent to mastery—at a time when her mastery supplied a pivotal link in the evolution of technology we take for granted today.

In Ada's time, and to a lesser degree in our own, certain skills were considered manly—and as such, beyond a woman's abilities. Since she was the daughter of the great Lord Byron, society might readily have assumed that her genetic gifts would place her among the great British women poets: the Brontë sisters, Rossetti, and George Eliot. Ada could have succumbed to assumptions driven by her father's reputation and allowed his fame to stand in for her own talents. But the prejudices and expectations of her time were no match for Ada. Consciously or not, she adhered to her father's belief that adversity is the first path to truth. She recognized that she possessed skills that flew in the face of convention, but would not allow expectations or societal norms to derail her from her own authentic path toward relevance.

Each of us has the raw ability to achieve mastery, but the path of the master requires an ethic that emphasizes character over personality. Merely maintaining the appearance of skill will not carry us to mastery or relevancy. In order to offer value, our skills must be proved through a disciplined process of deliberate, regular practice. An eye for color does not constitute a painter any more than nimble hands constitute a heart surgeon. Raw signature strengths matter, but they must be developed through the trial and error of constant practical application. Once we see our core assets with clarity, we are ready to embark on the process of developing them. Personal mastery goes beyond competence and skills; it is an approach that views day-to-day life as an ongoing committed practice of our skills.

POETRY IN A WHOLE NEW KIND OF LANGUAGE.

Ada was the only child of Byron's single marriage; the couple split when Ada was barely a month old and Byron never saw his daughter again. The girl was a clever but lonely prodigy, possessed of her mother's unconventional aptitudes. At 12, Ada determined to invent a method of flying. She studied Euclid on her own. Her mother saw to it that she was well educated; with her remarkable talent and drive to learn, Ada quickly outpaced her tutors. She was reputed to have been a vivacious and confident young woman, with talents that reached beyond courtly niceties to embrace a much rarer strength: a first-rate mind. At 17, she met Charles Babbage, a mathematical engineer with a passion for technical innovation. The meeting made a lasting impression on both of them.

Under her mother's social guidance, Ada married an aristocrat who eventually was elevated to earl of Lovelace, making Ada a countess. In many ways, she led the typical life of 19th-century nobility, but she never forgot the kinship she felt with Babbage. A friend of both Babbage and Ada's mother began to tutor Ada. Under his direction, Ada's talents, enhanced by her creative imagination, unfolded in the development of a brilliant mind. She went on to study under world-class thinkers, including the Scottish astronomer Mary Somerville, the first woman admitted into the Royal Astronomical Society. When all the world expected Ada to move through her days with social grace, she stepped beyond expectations and took on one of the most challenging problems of her age.

Along her path to mastery, Ada was not simply learning what she needed to know to make her way in the world; she was engaged in learning that enhanced her capacity to create. The joy of creative learning embraces basic principles that cultivate the practice of mastery and guide us toward a relevant life:

- **A sense of purpose to guide our goals.**
- **A vision that is a calling, as opposed to a motivation that merely seems like "just a good idea at the time."**
- **An outlook in which current reality is an ally, not an enemy.**

- A commitment to an accurate understanding of reality.
- An inquisitive approach to life.
- A resolution to work with change, versus resisting change.
- A sense that we are connected to life and to others.
- An emphasis on influencing, versus controlling, our environment.

ENGLISH TO ITALIAN AND BACK AGAIN.

We see these principles at work in Ada's collaboration with Babbage, who had conceived what many regard as the first programmable computer. Babbage called it the "Analytical Engine" and hoped to use it to perform complex mathematical calculations. Ada viewed his work on display in his drawing room and grasped in his prototype the beauty of the abstractions she loved. His inventiveness stirred in her a sense of purpose and a vision for what she might accomplish. This was no fleeting interest; Ada's letters afterward continued to reference Babbage and her fascination with his machine.

When England failed to give Babbage's invention its visionary due, he presented it in Italy. A young Italian mathematician wrote a scientific report introducing Babbage's machine—in Italian. This report reached Ada. Sensing an opportunity to learn, Ada translated the paper herself, without telling Babbage. Compelled by her own interest and curiosity, Ada expanded on the paper as she translated, to give a fuller explanation of how Babbage's machine worked. When she shared her translation with Babbage, the collaboration between the now-27-year-old countess and the 51-year-old technical visionary took enthusiastic flight. Ada's passion for Babbage's "Analytical Engine" forged a connection between them, and opened for Ada an opportunity to influence the invention's development.

By this point in Ada's education, she had achieved mastery of the gift that Babbage needed most: meticulous mathematical expertise. Babbage was a genius at designing a computer (punch cards and all), but he didn't have the skill to program it. He turned to Ada, the one person who had demonstrated that she really understood his work. The young countess created what is considered the first algorithm ever specifically tailored for implementation on a computer. Her work, combined with Babbage's, would enable computers to calculate extremely difficult Bernoulli numbers.

THE U.S. ARMY SALUTES ADA.

Today, Ada is acknowledged as one of the founders of scientific computing and the first computer programmer. The U.S. Army named a computer language after her, and the British Computer Society regularly awards a medal in Ada's name. Around the world, scholarships, computer centers, and events pay her homage. Her determination to master her gifts, regardless of the adversity of class expectations, gender stereotypes, and the narcotic of perpetual comfort, won her more relevance in history's eyes than the elegant lives of a thousand counts and countesses combined. Her commitment to mastery has transformed our modern way of living.

As Ada's accomplishments attest, mastery is not a landmark we reach; it is a personal practice of ongoing discipline. Ada's talent was not realized in one grand unveiling of an "aha!" moment. The algorithm she crafted was the result of slow meticulous work over time. With the practice of mastery comes the gradual realization that fulfillment is not defined by the moments when our efforts are rewarded; rather, fulfillment is the joy we take in the day-to-day experience of living a life of personal meaning in pursuit of our authentic interests.

Nurturing the pursuit of mastery in daily life requires discipline that is not cultivated by the instant-gratification pace of the modern world. As Aristotle observed centuries ago: "Excellence is never an accident. It is always the result of high intention, sincere effort, and intelligent execution; it represents the wise choice among many alternatives—choice, not chance, determines your destiny."

PRACTICE, PRACTICE, PRACTICE.

In her book *Mindset*, Stanford psychologist Carol Dweck explains that making mistakes, and learning from them, is critical to the development of mastery. It is by focusing on errors and carefully analyzing our decision-making process that we improve our skills, bit by bit, over time. Dweck's theory is based on decades of research demonstrating that the ability to learn from mistakes is crucial to successful learning. Dweck designed a learning experiment for more than 400 fifth-graders. She discovered that how children are praised dramatically affects their future performance. When children were praised for their innate intelligence, they perceived "being smart" as an asset to be guarded, and they shied away from challenges that might threaten their status. Instead, when given a choice between an easier or more challenging task, the "smart" children chose to bolster their self-esteem by sticking with tasks they were confident that they could master, and compared themselves to the children who had performed worse. These children focused on documenting their intelligence instead of developing it. They acted on the belief that success was a matter of innate talent and did not require effort.

On the other hand, children praised for their effort—their willingness to work hard—gravitated toward the more challenging tasks. The "hard workers" took mistakes in stride, and were so eager to learn from their mistakes that they preferred to compare their performance to that of children who had done better than they had. These children acted on the belief that intelligence and talent were abilities developed through dedication and hard work. Their "growth mindset," to use Dweck's term, created a love of learning and a resilience that are essential to accomplishment. Because they were encouraged to challenge themselves, the "hardworking" children ended up performing at much higher levels than the children praised for intelligence. Dweck's conclusion? The most useful kinds of learning activities are the activities that encourage us to learn from our mistakes.

WISDOM—A SANE VIEW OF SELF.

Talent is a necessary but not a sufficient quality on the road to mastery. In order to master our gifts, we have to be willing to take risks, to fail, and to learn from our failures. Constructive self-criticism and self-improvement give us a deep understanding of how a complex interplay of factors may affect a specific situation. When Phil interviews candidates for positions in his company, he always leads with the same question: "Tell me the single time when you've been most broken in your life. How did you respond? What did you learn?"

If the candidate cannot answer, Phil goes no further. He isn't looking for candidates who are merely smart. As he will tell you, there are a million smart people. He is looking for wisdom, and he knows that most wisdom comes from adversity and the resilience to respond and learn. He has learned that success is failure's progeny. The willingness to learn from failure bolsters a clear understanding of our core skills and an interface between wisdom and aptitude, which introduces another facet to the understanding of mastery: saneness.

Personal saneness, in the context of mastery, is the wisdom to leverage our skill set while simultaneously being in touch with our limitations. Like authenticity, mastery is less a destination than a path on which we advance over time. We are more skilled today than we were yesterday, but we are not as skilled now as we will be tomorrow.

We may wish we had a silver bullet to conquer the heady goals to which we aspire; but we don't believe that mastery is a perfection target to be reached. Mastery is a process. There is always room to improve. The sane view of self is a balance between aspirations and limitations. It is an understanding of what is appropriate, informed by the boundaries of our mastery.

YOU-ER THAN YOU.

The Cat in the Hat is Tom and Phil's contemporary, and they are grateful for this. Their fathers were not whimsical men, and yet the charming rhymes, inventive words, and preposterous illustrations of Theodor Geisel, better known as Dr. Seuss, made their fathers readily volunteer when it came time to read to their rambunctious sons.

Tom and Phil, in turn, spent a great deal of time reading Dr. Seuss to their own children. This second introduction to Dr. Seuss gave them the opportunity to discover a completely different dimension of Geisel's work. There was a lot of truth in what he had to say. There is one line in Geisel's *Happy Birthday to You!* that Tom would be willing to tattoo on his forearm—if he weren't so afraid of needles:

Today you are you. That is truer than true.
There is no one alive who is you-er than you.

Mastery requires that we focus on owning and celebrating our authentic selves—our "you-ness." As we consider Geisel's work today, we realize his playfully clever stories reveal a deeper truth about the unique authenticity at the core of each of us, and they also reflect the truth of Geisel's own story. He lived a life that embraced and practiced his own singular verbal mastery.

When an education study was published in the 1950s damning the Dick and Jane primers as ineffective reading tools for children, William Spaulding, then director of Houghton Mifflin's education division, invited Geisel to dinner. Spaulding dared Geisel to write a story that would captivate first-graders. Nine months later, Geisel came back with *The Cat in the Hat*. His utterly unique voice demonstrated what children's education could be, and the book sold a million copies within five years.

Being you-er than you requires that we scrape off the barnacles that stick to us when we try to imitate others and begin focusing on our own distinctive set of gifts. When we develop mastery around our own gifts, it's like going from being out of shape to being physically fit—same you, only better.

BE THE NEXT GREAT YOU.

A few years ago, a firm approached Tom's agency, Riley Hayes, with a merger proposition. Part of their pitch was "Together we will be the next Fallon." They were referring to the most meteoric agency ever to come from the Twin Cities. Fallon is still one of the finest practitioners of the craft in the advertising world. Tempting as it was to imagine claiming such heady accolades, Tom knew that although imitation might be flattering, it wasn't authentic. Fallon's path to mastery was a path that honed Fallon's superlative skills. Perhaps the merger slogan could have been "Just like Fallon, but not quite as good!" Who needs another Fallon when there is a perfectly good Fallon open for business and going strong? Although Riley Hayes aspired to their own definition of greatness, Tom also had a realistic understanding of his company's limitations, and he knew this opportunity was not their authentic path. Riley Hayes declined the merger offer, and the merger eventually transpired with another agency. As successful as the merged agencies have been, no one has ever called them the next Fallon.

Honoring the principles of mastery is a balancing act of sorts. Specifically, we learn to balance aspirations, realizations, and limitations. This can be challenging in a world overwhelmed by complexity and compelled to achieve perfection. Throughout our careers, we have seen how accomplished, significant professionals have fallen into the temptation of trying to become something they are not. Admittedly, we've fallen into this trap ourselves.

IMITATION IS THE SPEEDIEST FORM OF FALTERING.

In *The Greater Journey*, his fascinating history of Americans in Paris between 1830 and 1900, author David McCullough chronicles the ambitions of physicians, artists, and writers whose achievements abroad changed the course of American history. Interestingly, painters including John Singer Sargent and

Mary Cassatt spent long hours at the Louvre, imitating the work of the masters they admired. These artists employed imitation in order to strengthen their skills, but they weren't striving to become expert forgers of another artist's style. They used the expertise they developed as a foundation for creating their own signature styles. As Henri Matisse observed, "An artist must ... prepare the mastery which will later enable him to express himself in his own language." For these artists, imitation was a means of learning, not a means of being.

NICE WORK IF YOU CAN GET IT.

It is a valuable lesson for us to remember. Legendary Broadway composer George Gershwin was famous for his admiration of classical music. After attending orchestra concerts, Gershwin would go to his piano and attempt to replicate what he had heard. He is rumored to have asked composers Maurice Ravel and Arnold Schoenberg for lessons. As the stories go, Ravel responded, "Why be a second-rate Ravel when you are a first-rate Gershwin?" In similar vein, Schoenberg is said to have replied, "I would only make you a bad Schoenberg, and you're such a good Gershwin already." Factually accurate or not, these charming anecdotes reflect the lessons of authenticity and mastery: better to be yourself than to imitate the best self of someone else.

In our own time, there is an impulse to chase perfection by following the lead of the best someone else full tilt toward the next victory. It is difficult to resist sidelong assessments of our competitors' successes, or the temptation to duplicate their success by trying to remold ourselves in their image. They have 10,000 social media fans? We need 10,000 fans. They sit on six boards? We should too. Imitation can seem easier than invention, but it will not put us on the path of relevance.

GOLIATH DOES A BAD DAVID IMITATION.

In the late 1990s, Riley Hayes was hired to work on a large account that was serviced predominantly by an agency 30 times the size of Tom's agency. The client was not considering Riley Hayes to take over the account; they had only been hired to keep this rival agency's estimates and timelines honest. Of course, outnumbered though Riley Hayes was, taking over the account was exactly what they set out to do. Soon, the rival started to panic. In the heat of competition, they did a strategically foolish thing. Instead of focusing on how they could use their unique skills to further hone the quality of their account service, they rushed to imitate what Riley Hayes did best. The rival agency went to the client and asked, "How can we be more like Riley Hayes?" They tried to mimic an agency one-thirtieth their size, just to win more of the work than they already had. They abandoned their own strengths and tried to imitate the strengths of Riley Hayes. You can predict the result. Ultimately, they lost the account, and Riley Hayes replaced them as the agency of record.

PATHS TO MASTERY.

As we work with our clients, we see a compulsive drive to reproduce proofs of success. It is not an instinct that serves us well—there is no surer way to commoditization than by attempting to ape your competitor. Appearing to be just like someone else is no substitute for claiming and developing the self that only we can claim. Unless our compass is grounded in authenticity, mastery will elude us and we will find ourselves among the indistinguishable and the commoditized.

SHORTCUTS MAKE FOR LONG JOURNEYS.

Mastery is not a quick-fix solution. The frantic pace of today's world, and the desire for quick, highly visible results, is one of the most predictable ways to sabotage mastery. Mastery is a slow and steady practice; it is not a pell-mell race to a finish line.

Today's world is media savvy, option rich, information-based, skeptical, and impatient. These are not conditions conducive to the practice of mastery. Yet, how we show up is our only sustainable distinguisher. More and more frequently, it is not our solution that distinguishes us; it's our ability to show up in a way that thwarts the expectations of the status quo and commands attention. When we show up as our authentic selves, we demonstrate our unique value in a world filled with look-alike commoditized voices. To put it in very simple terms, how is the new why.

We observe clients whose daily schedules are booked from breakfast conferences through dinner meetings; any fleeting moments in between are consumed by phone calls and emails. There is no time to reflect on whether the mass of daily decisions is moving us constructively toward our larger objectives or contributing to our mastery of authentic skills. We speed along in thrall to the perfection myth, which dictates that accomplishment lies in measuring how much we have closed the gap between the person we are and the ideal person we want to be. When we are so busy measuring how far we have to go, it is easy to lose sight of who we want to be.

MAJORING IN THE MAJORS.

The key to life is to major in the majors, not to major in the minors. Because the engine of distraction looms so large in today's world, it has never been more difficult to major in the majors, or more easy to major in the minors. In today's global state of permanent, compulsive distraction and epidemic complexity fatigue, it is no small challenge to establish a firm foundation for mastery.

The sheer volume of complexity, Internet, and media generates an enormous attraction to the trivial. The cornerstones of mastery won't stand fast in the trivial. We might become really good at things that don't matter, but majoring in the minors is not going to help us develop the valued skills that distinguish us in a commoditized world.

In order to combat trivial distractions, we first have to recognize them. The symptoms of distraction are easy to identify when we know what to look for. They include:

- **Addiction to activity.**

- **A mental state of constant emergency overload.**

- **The compulsion to avail ourselves of the excess of access that technology provides.**

- **The emotional absence of individuals engrossed in the screens of their devices while oblivious to their immediate surroundings.**

We ride in cars and trains and planes together, join friends over coffee or a meal, and sit in meetings—with our focus on the glowing screen in our hands and not on the faces of the people around us. One of our deep concerns with social media is its seductiveness. People can create online lives that infuse their cyber identities with more importance than their real-life identities. When energy is dedicated to a simulated self, or invested in the digital world, meaningful face-to-face interactions suffer. As society becomes more isolated, we sense electronic connection growing hand in hand with relational disconnection. This makes the ability to connect with relevancy suddenly much more rare and attractive than ever.

STROLLING TOWARD MASTERY.

Slowing down to address the pressures of complexity opens opportunities to review and assess our beliefs, and to reconnect with our authentic self. These are exactly the practices that build mastery. Moving at light speed makes us vulnerable to error. There is no time to analyze the errors we do make, and learn from them. When winning becomes the only focus, there's no room to value practice and discipline. If we don't take risks and fail, we lose the crucial lessons that failure has to teach us.

When we speed to our goal, we run the risk of reacting to surface symptoms instead of looking for underlying information, patterns, and issues. Anyone who has attended an auction has experienced firsthand the fast-paced fever to win. The rapid-fire tempo of competitive bidding is seductive. It allows no time for reflection. It is easy to be caught up in the rush and not realize until after the auctioneer's hammer comes down that we've offered a ridiculous sum for an object that seemed desirable only in the heat of the bidding moment. Successful bidders have mastered resistance to the seduction of the auction atmosphere. They plan their strategy before they pick up their paddles, and they've learned to keep their quiet concentration and resist the escalating rhythm of the auctioneer.

THE BALANCE BETWEEN ASPIRATION, EXPECTATION, AND LIMITATION.

In the quest for mastery, focus matters. There's no doubt that setting aspirations is a great start to achieving success. It's necessary to plot our journey with our objective in mind. When we have identified the skills we want to master, we can plan the action steps we'll need to take in order to achieve our goals.

But we think there's a catch to this formula. When high aspirations are tied to equally high expectations, there's a risk that we'll be caught in the pressure to constantly chase our own demanding expectations. If our focus is always on that bar we can't quite reach, mastery shifts from being a consistently rewarding practice to being a constantly moving finish line. It's easy to forget to pause. It's easy to lose sight of the fact that our limitations are opportunities for us to learn more. Caught in a race to succeed, we don't allow ourselves to stop and consider the reasons for our mistakes. We lose the opportunity to improve. Combining high aspirations and high expectations is a formula for exhaustion and frustration. When we are always focused on the distance we have yet to travel, we don't give ourselves the reflective time to savor the journey and appreciate the progress we've already made.

UNREALISTIC ASPIRATIONS PLUS CRAZY EXPECTATIONS EQUAL EXTREME EXASPERATION.

An intriguing trait being identified in business may point to one way to avoid the aspiration/expectation trap. This emerging trait is called learning agility, and it is characterized by the speed and willingness with which we learn new competencies and adapt our thinking and behavior to the challenge before us. People with learning agility are able to analyze a situation from multiple perspectives, adjusting their approach as they go, even if this means pushing beyond their preferred style. Agile learners exhibit critical thinking skills and the insight to leverage their strengths. They are comfortable with the discomfort of change. Although these learners love to achieve, they do not pursue achievement single-mindedly. They place a higher priority on learning and improvement than they do on success. And a value system in which learning is preeminent makes the agile learner an excellent role model for mastery.

When we make learning a priority, we move forward with our attention divided between the challenges ahead and the personal growth we achieve through assessment. We learn as we go, with our focus balanced between past lessons and future aspirations. We are much more likely to feel satisfaction with every step of the journey.

THE GOOD NEWS IS THAT YOU WILL
NEVER GET THERE.

Life isn't destinational—it's transitional. We describe the mindset of mastery as a permanent sense of never-arrivedness, and this definition is a great defense against the danger of assuming that we have a corner on the truth. When we have a comfort level with feeling unfinished, we are cultivating a state of intentional ambiguity. This constantly invites growth into our life.

Embracing learning agility prompts us to prioritize the ongoing discipline of mastery over the brass ring of accolades. We are aware of the limits of our knowledge. Our self-confidence regarding our competencies is balanced by self-honesty regarding our shortcomings. We won't allow unrealistic expectations to govern our behavior, and we maintain a sense of transitional thinking.

Beliefs drive decisions, decisions drive behaviors, and behaviors become practices. Mastery invites us to define a personal vision and a personal life purpose. It asks us to live with an objective, accurate view of ourselves. When we practice mastery, goals become moving targets to be continually clarified and redefined as we pause to assess our progress. We hold creative tension between our vision for the future and our current reality. We have a vision for the contribution we hope to make, but we also take the time to appreciate how far we have come. We find ourselves embracing curiosity and becoming more inquisitive. Because mastery is committed to the truth, we align our personal values with time-honored principles of honesty, integrity, and discipline. Mastery is a way for us to strive to be the best version of ourselves. This is a lifelong journey, dedicated to tapping our full potential as a human being and to applying our skills appropriately in the service of others.

IT'S BETTER NOT TO SAIL THAN BAIL.

Tom has lived on the water for most of his life; understanding of water is in his genes. He is a strong swimmer and an excellent boatman. He canoes, sails, and kayaks. If he's in a strange boat, he can figure it out. Tom understands his element, practices the skills that water sports require, and knows when to apply them. But he is also wise enough to recognize when his skills are no match for the elements. A part of his mastery lies in knowing when to stay off the water—he respects his limitations. When Lake Superior turns stormy, Tom knows that it's time to bring the boat in. When water temperatures hover around freezing, he knows it's too dangerous to go out and risk an accident in extremely cold conditions. There are dangerous situations that are beyond our control; honoring them is a part of what defines mastery.

Slowing down gives us the time to remember the tools that are core to our skill set, and to reflect on whether we are using them wisely. Complexity is best addressed by slowing down to take a personal inventory, reconnect with our signature strengths, reflect on whether we are making sane and appropriate use of those strengths, and then make the adjustments we need to make in order to balance the energy of aspiration with the wisdom of sane limitation.

Mastery is about understanding the context in which we excel. That context becomes our authentic promise—a promise that is as important to individuals as it is to companies and products. Our promise reflects both our strengths and our limitations. An honest inventory enables us to see ourselves in an accurate way.

Our definition of personal mastery encompasses three components:

• **Our skill set: identifying the strengths that are unique to us.**

• **Our mindset: the courage and consistency to keep our eyes on the path.**

• **Our experience set: the lessons we learn through the practice of our skills.**

Mastery benefits from a mindset that understands the balance between aspiration, expectation, and limitation. Every time we interact, in any context, we exude a promise that tells people who we are. When we make it our goal to deliver a dependable promise that accurately defines who we are, our actions reflect both our authenticity and our talents. People want to contract with real human beings who listen, tell the truth, and follow through. Service rooted in authenticity is one of the great sustainable distinguishers. Cultivating realistic and dependable expectations requires us to understand our authentic self, choose the disciplined path of mastery, and seize the lessons that enable us to continually refine our skills.

TIN PANNING FOR GOLD.

There is a contemporary perspective that suggests that creative mastery—especially in the arts—grows best unfettered by boundaries and restrictions. Artists speak longingly of the too few projects that allow them free rein to express themselves. The implication is that creative genius is squashed by limitations; we reach our richest potential when the sky's the limit and imagination runs free.

Or do we?

Admittedly, Gershwin would probably be bowled over by modern digital technology. Today as never before, artistic control is in the hands of composers and performers. Most musicians have access to recording hardware and software that enables them to bypass expensive studios, record music at home, and distribute it online, with no censoring record label looking over their shoulders to direct—or restrict—creativity. Some artists own their own publishing companies and promote themselves on social media at little or no cost. Our music industry operates in a zenith of self-expression.

But this creative freedom is a relatively recent development. During the Renaissance, Baroque, and Classical periods, a musician's livelihood depended on the patronage of the aristocracies and churches. Artists worked within defined themes and deadlines, and if patrons were not pleased, the penalties could be severe. This was hardly a formula for uninhibited artistic expression, yet these eras produced classical masterpieces of musical genius by composers including Johann Sebastian Bach, Handel, Vivaldi, and Mozart.

More recent history also suggests that musical mastery can flourish within the discipline of confined framework. In the late 1800s, a group of music publishers and songwriters congregated along West 28th Street between Fifth and Sixth avenues in Manhattan. The metallic cacophony of dueling upright pianos in the publishers' offices prompted the district's nickname: Tin Pan Alley. The musicians of the day understood their market. They were composing for people who bought sheet music that they could play and enjoy on the parlor piano at home. Sheet music specifications may not have been dictated by kings and popes, but presented equally restrictive challenges. Composers could write music in only a handful of keys. The structure allowed 32 bars and a set format of verses and choruses with one bridge. Producing music within these limitations required tremendous discipline.

For the songwriters of Tin Pan Alley, unfettered conditions didn't exist. If they wanted their music to sell, there was no choice but to conform to the dictates of printed music that could be performed by amateur musicians. No songwriters since have composed within such constraints, but this pragmatic enclave of American musicians demonstrated what is possible in the dynamic tension between aspiration and discipline.

Out of the cacophony of sheet music tunes composed on cheap upright pianos in a corner of Manhattan emerged a new style of American music, written by some of our country's most celebrated composers: Irving Berlin, Cole Porter, and George Gershwin. Working within the restrictions of their era, these composers and their colleagues produced timeless standards that have won an enduring place in the fabric of American music. Their work is a testament to creativity that flourishes in spite of, or perhaps because of, the impediments that inspire mastery to triumph.

Mastery doesn't require perfect conditions in order to fully flex its potential; the conditions only have to be perfect enough. As the Tin Pan Alley musicians demonstrate, a gateway to opportunity is enough. Mastery can flourish even when opportunity's road winds through a forest of restrictions and limitations.

THE PITFALLS OF PERFECTION.

Waiting for the perfect moment and the perfect conditions is a trap. The desire for perfection can be a siren song, and like the ensorcelling melodies of the mythic Greek sirens that lured sailors to shipwreck, perfection as a goal can lead to a tragic conclusion. When we seek perfection in everything, we cannot attain it in anything.

We've found it more powerful to reframe perfection. Instead of viewing it as a goal, we see it as a compass point along the journey. At any point, we can assess our current state in terms of both how far we have come and how far we still want to go. Our current state is where we are—a statement of achievement, in comparison to where we were before. The progress we intend to make toward our goal informs us about the tasks that lie ahead. By focusing on both the gains we've made and the gains we intend to make, we have an aspirational promise to ourselves that is tethered to reality.

THE CONSISTENCY OF CLARITY.

When we are certain of our context and our signature strengths, we know which tasks we can handle competently, and which tasks we need to outsource. Effective and reliable communication requires clarity of focus and a confident understanding of self. That knowledge informs what we know as saneness—realistic aspiration balanced by limitations that we acknowledge with courageous clarity. These are the qualities that will elevate a personal authenticity to valued relevance.

MASTERY AND HAPPINESS.

There is one more element that strengthens our commitment to mastery and is critical to the value of our authentic promise: happiness. We can have all the clarity in the world, understand our signature strengths, and develop a personal brand, but if we aren't fundamentally happy, we have nothing to give and little motivation to improve. Unhappiness depletes our energy. In our experience, valuing earned success contributes significantly to happiness.

We define earned success as achievement based on merit and hard work. We have a deep belief in the value of work. Psychologists, negotiators, and even dating coaches will tell us that the value we place on something is related to the effort we have invested to earn it. Good things that are not earned don't increase a person's sense of well-being. A negotiator will feel more successful if she perceives that she wrested a valuable concession from the party on the other side of the table. The concessions she had to fight for will be prized more than those that were readily offered up. We value what we earn more than we value what is given to us. Earned success allows us to measure our life's profit in our own terms, be it money, making music, or helping people.

The dynamics that can undercut our capacity for happiness and our commitment to mastery are just as important to understand. They include entitlement, learned helplessness, and comparison.

ENTITLEMENT.

Entitlement is the attitude that asserts mastery without possessing the portfolio of accomplishments to support the claim. We may want to own a MacBook Pro—but some of us might say that obtaining this object of desire depends upon our cash reserves or other factors that we may or may not control. We don't feel entitled to the latest laptop iteration; we understand that this is something we have to earn. Others want to own that MacBook regardless of their circumstances. Because they want it, it should be theirs, they reason. They feel entitled to a new MacBook Pro, viewing it as an object they simply deserve to have.

Entitlement removes discipline from the equation. For the entitled, neither mastery nor happiness are viewed as earned rewards achieved through committed effort. Desiring something through the lens of entitlement results in one of two possible outcomes, neither of which leads to happiness. Either we get the MacBook Pro and then fret that we didn't get it as soon as we deserved it, or we don't get it and gnaw over the injustice of being denied what should have been ours. Either way, entitlement bars the door to feelings of gratitude and short-circuits the motivations that develop mastery. There is no incentive to develop our skills if we are already convinced that rewards are our just due.

LEARNED HELPLESSNESS.

Mastery can be sabotaged by the self-doubt of learned helplessness just as surely as it can be derailed by an attitude of overconfident entitlement. Learned helplessness defines a neurological response triggered by the belief that nothing we do will make a difference and that our efforts won't work to bring us what we want. If we believe that failure or disappointment is inevitable and permanent, we will not take action to try to change our circumstances.

Researchers have found that not everyone reacts with helplessness in difficult circumstances. Some people never give up, no matter what. At the opposite end of the spectrum, there are people who begin life with feelings of helplessness— it does not take any experience with uncontrollability at all to make them give up.

Why are some people impervious to helplessness? Researchers have discovered that when people identified their strengths and devoted themselves to developing mastery of them, they were less likely to be discouraged by setbacks. Many people think that a genius is someone who never fails, someone for whom everything magically works. This could not be further from the truth. Every genius suffers the birthing pains of the creative process, gets stuck in dead ends, takes wrong turns, and perseveres despite these setbacks. Irving Stone titled his biography of Michelangelo *The Agony and the Ecstasy*. He understood that mastery demands both the agony of failure and the ecstasy of creation accomplished. Authenticity and mastery breed strength and resilience. We combat the demoralization of fearing that we don't matter with an approach to living that we call earned success.

THE DANGER OF THE UNATTAINABLE AND THE ARBITRARY.

When we measure ourselves against the impossible standard of perfection, we will always find ourselves wanting. Phil's wife, Julie, saw firsthand the damage that can be caused by unattainable expectations. Through her 25-year teaching career, Julie worked with too many students who tragically developed anorexia in attempts to conform their bodies to digitally retouched and idealized media portrayals of size 0 models and movie stars. When these young girls compared themselves to the unattainable image that they believed they were supposed to be, their fixation was frustratingly difficult to challenge. In the case of this terrible disorder, the consequences of chasing perfection can be deadly. Eating disorders have the highest mortality rate of any mental illness. Even when the ramifications are less severe, a compulsion to pursue the unattainable can push both happiness and mastery out of reach.

How do we pursue mastery without falling into the trap of measuring ourselves against unattainable ideals? We have identified two ways to gauge mastery that provide valuable and positive feedback. A healthy assessment of mastery considers both:

• **The level of skill we possess.**

• **An appreciation for how far we've come in our skill development compared to where we were in the past.**

A sous-chef with dreams of her own restaurant empire may have mastered the art of classical French sauce making, but not yet have developed the signature cooking style she imagines as the cornerstone of her own chain of restaurants. She gauges her progress not only by whether she is moving toward her aspirations, but also by her improving skills. Our chef may not yet have the stature of Chef Auguste Escoffier or Emeril Lagasse, but she can remember a time when she could not name the five French mother sauces, let alone execute them. She's made progress. Appreciating the skills she has developed is a marker along the path toward her culinary aspirations. The sense of accomplishment that accompanies improved skills is one of the rewards we reap when we dedicate ourselves to mastery.

CHOOSING PROGRESS OVER PERFECTION.

At any point in the journey, we may not be where we want to be, but have we progressed from where we were before? Asking this question helps us to remind ourselves that mastery is an incremental journey fueled by curiosity and passion; it is not a sprint to a defined finish line. The American physicist Richard Feynman expressed the master's approach when he explained that he didn't enjoy physics equations because they were important for the future of science; he enjoyed them because they were interesting and amusing. This scientist who loved to do physics "without worrying about any importance whatsoever" is ranked as one of the 10 greatest physicists of all times.

In his autobiography, *Surely You're Joking, Mr. Feynman!* he explains that his Nobel Prize was the result of a decision to play with physics for his own entertainment. While in the cafeteria at the university where he taught, he watched a guy throw a plate in the air. The plate wobbled. Intrigued, Feynman set about figuring out the motion of the rotating plate. When one of his colleagues asked him why he was bothering with a wobbly plate, Feynman responded, "I'm just doing it for the fun of it." Feynman's curiosity with wobbly plates and their rotation rates—a curiosity born of inquisitive pleasure—led to the discoveries that won him Nobel Prize recognition.

Feynman was motivated by his pleasure with physics. He had uncovered his authentic gifts and pursued them for the enjoyment they brought him. When we take pleasure in our skills on a path of continuous progress, we are truly living a life of mastery. When we adopt the habit of balancing progress thinking with aspirational thinking, we dodge the traps of the unattainable and the arbitrary, and experience the satisfaction of pursuing mastery for the pleasure it gives us. Genuine mastery is a progressive path that is measured step by step, and day by day.

Our observations about mastery suggest that a constructive perspective embraces high aspirations in conjunction with a sane view of our limitations, and an understanding that the world owes us nothing. Learned helplessness can be prevented by teaching people that their actions do make a difference, and can be cured by teaching people to view setbacks as temporary and not permanent. In the same way, even our errors, when viewed as learning opportunities, are indications of growth, rather than failure. We never know what might be waiting for us around the next bend in the road, or what discovery a failure might reveal.

PERSONAL MASTERY.

Building our personal mastery gives us choices. Identifying core skills grounds us and shows us where to pursue mastery. We carry our portfolio of qualities and skills with us on a journey of individual, personal, and continuous improvement. Life provides an abundance of opportunities for growth; choosing wisely among them is a matter of understanding our strengths and limitations—and our worldview.

The habits of mastery are ours to develop:

- Discipline

- Proactivity

- Focus

- Ordered priorities

- Courageous clarity

When we sit down with clients to help them define the "one thing" around which to build their authentic promise, we present it as a process of figuring out how to help them move forward in mastering the service or product they provide. Authenticity in combination with mastery enables individuals and companies to articulate a dependable promise to those they wish to serve. We have the deep understanding, we have the skills, and we have the wisdom. The test of our promise's authenticity can be evaluated through four components:

- The promise must be a reflection of our unique self.

- The promise must be meaningful; it must reflect the truth well told.

- The promise must represent a brand of one.

- The promise must reflect a balance of character and competence.

Mastery is an accurate understanding of our situation, and having the skills to survive and thrive in a particular environment. With awareness of our gifts tempered by a sane view of self, we have the grounding we need to set out on the journey to personal success. Mastery is about understanding what is in our control and what is not.

NATURAL REWARDS.

As we assume the habits of mastery, we change, we grow, and we continue our practice through periods of plateau until we work our way to another level of improvement. Mastery demands change, and change requires both time and energy. On the path of mastery, we cultivate the discipline to skirt distractions and give up the time-wasters that deter us from our objectives. The pursuit of mastery is challenging, but it is a journey that does not go unrewarded.

Unconscious competence. Whenever we begin to hone a new skill or attempt a new project, we are not even conscious of what we don't know. Our mistakes point out the areas where we need to improve. With practice, we can identify the knowledge we need to acquire—we become conscious of our shortcomings. At this stage, dedication is crucial. We must stick to our studies, acquiring experience and practicing our skills until, gradually, over time, our mastery becomes unconscious habit. As long as we remain focused on mastering our skills, we can confidently attain unconscious competence in our lives.

Living a "joy now" versus "joy later" life. Mastery balances a sane view of self with aspiration and limitation, and this balance is key to avoiding the trap of pursuing joy that waits perpetually just around the next bend in the road. The practice of mastery invites us to revel in each step of our progress even as we pursue new lessons that will take us even further.

Living in the present. When we identify our talents and focus with clarity on our goals, we know what we need to do, and we are more likely to pour our energy into work that helps us achieve more relevance in our world. Relevance requires us to take action in the present—and makes it easier to resist distractions. Mastery asks us to make a conscious effort to be emotionally present in our lives, rewarding us with joys "in the moment" that we would otherwise have missed.

Pursuit of your noble purpose. Not everyone has encountered a Great Humbling, but many of us have encountered life situations that have challenged us or introduced us to the concept that the world is larger than we originally imagined. The experience spurs new awareness and a desire to hone our talents in the service of others. Mastery gives us the power to claim a noble purpose; it encourages us to take risks in life, and to live a life of meaning and gratitude.

The currency of confidence. All of us have the potential to develop power over our authentic gifts. One of the benefits of mastery is the realization that difficulties can be overcome. Improving our skills is our choice. The discipline of regularly transforming experience into a source of growth breeds confidence and the courage to tackle new challenges.

Clarity breeds collaboration. With a sane view of self comes acceptance that we are not going to be good at everything. It can be a mutually beneficial pleasure to reach out to respected individuals who possess talents we lack. People committed to mastery of their own gifts recognize and respect others with the same value, and they frequently share support with generosity. By pooling resources in a group of multidisciplinary colleagues, we create a dynamic that enables us to share our talents.

"YOU" ARE THE ONLY THING YOU CAN BE REALLY GOOD AT.

Find out which tools are in the toolbox, and make the most of them. If our toolbox contains only a level and a plane, we aren't ever going to build a house. We might be able to hang a door just right, but constructing a house is beyond our abilities. We have to understand what we have.

Becoming the people we were meant to be is not just what we should be doing—it's probably the only option we have if we truly want to be great at something. Think about it. We all, by definition, have the perfect set of gifts to put into service on the path to becoming a uniquely better form of ourselves. Ada Lovelace followed her passion for mathematics even when her path breached the social boundaries for acceptably feminine occupations. She even envisioned the application of the computer to musical compositions, foretelling the digital technology that brings the timeless standards of Tin Pan Alley musicians into our homes today. Ada lived a brief 36 years before cancer claimed her life, and she made the most of them. Her contribution to computer technology underpins our modern lives and is a testament to the potential of a life lived on the path of mastery.

Babbage dubbed Ada "The Enchantress of Numbers." Her commitment to honing her authentic talents made her an enchantress with mastery over her rare mathematical gifts.

MASTERY SUMMARY INSIGHTS

If we hope to be relevant, we must be masterful at what we do.

The effect of mastery on our relevance is exponential.

The joy of learning embraces basic principles that cultivate mastery:
- *A sense of purpose to guide our goals.*
- *A vision that is a calling.*
- *An outlook in which current reality is an ally, not an enemy.*
- *A commitment to an accurate understanding of reality.*
- *An inquisitive approach to life.*
- *A resolution to work with change, versus resisting change.*
- *A sense that we are connected to life and to others.*
- *An emphasis on influencing, versus controlling, our environment.*

Wisdom—a sane view of self. A sane view of self is informed by the boundaries and limitations of our mastery.

You-er than you. Mastery asks us to abandon imitation and focus on our distinctive set of gifts. It's like going from being out of shape to physically fit—same you, only better.

Majoring in the majors. We must resist the enormous attraction to the trivial in order to lay the cornerstones of mastery.

In order to combat trivial distractions, we first have to recognize the symptoms of distraction:
- *Addiction to activity.*
- *A mental state of constant emergency overload.*
- *The compulsion to avail ourselves of the excess of access that technology provides.*

• *The emotional absence of individuals engrossed in devices while oblivious to their immediate surroundings.*

Our promise reflects both our strengths and our limitations. An honest inventory enables us to see ourselves accurately.

Our definition of personal mastery encompasses three components:
• *Our skill set: identifying the strengths that are unique to us.*
• *Our mindset: the courage and consistency to keep our eyes on the path.*
• *Our experience set: the lessons we learn through the practice of our skills.*

The habits of mastery are ours to develop:
• *Discipline*
• *Proactivity*
• *Focus*
• *Ordered priorities*
• *Courageous clarity*

Evaluate your promise's authenticity through four components:
• *The promise must be a reflection of your unique self.*
• *The promise must be meaningful; it must reflect the truth well told.*
• *The promise must represent a brand of one.*
• *The promise must reflect a balance of character and competence.*

The natural rewards of personal mastery include:
• **Unconscious competence.** *When we practice our skills, our mastery gradually becomes an unconscious habit.*
• **Living a "joy now" versus "joy later" life.** *Mastery balances a sane view of self with aspiration and limitation; it invites us to revel in each step of our progress.*
• **Living in the present.** *Mastery asks us to make a conscious effort to be emotionally present in our lives, rewarding us with joys "in the moment" that we would otherwise miss.*
• **Pursuit of your noble purpose.** *Mastery encourages us to take risks and live a life of noble purpose.*
• **The currency of confidence.** *Mastery is a source of growth that breeds confidence and the courage to tackle new challenges.*

- **Clarity breeds collaboration.** *With a sane view of self comes acceptance that we are not going to be good at everything. It is a mutually beneficial pleasure to pool resources with generosity.*
- **"You" are the only thing you can be really good at.** *It is our job to discover the tools in our own toolbox, and then make the most of them.*

Being good at something is only important if it is good for someone. With empathy, we match our mastery with the needs of others for whom we will matter more.

EMPATHY

$$(A_u + M^2 + \mathbf{E}) \times (A_c) = R$$

We're authentic and we have mastery. How do we make our skills relevant to others? Empathy. Think of empathy as the docking station of relevance. The ability to understand people's needs allows us to connect what we do with those who need it, and bring them the right thing at the right time. While there are many definitions for empathy, we love the clear articulation of this concept expressed by Harper Lee in *To Kill a Mockingbird*: "You never really understand a person until you consider things from his point of view, until you climb into his skin and walk around in it."

Before we can explore the role of empathy in relevance, we need a clear definition of what empathy is and what it is not. Originating from the Greek *empatheia*, meaning "passion," empathy's present meaning is a translation of the German word *Einfühlung* (from ein "in" plus fühlung "feeling"). Empathy is about being in the feeling of another—and this is distinct from sympathy. Sympathy is the expression of a feeling of pity and sorrow for someone else's misfortune. To be sympathetic is to acknowledge another's hardship, but that is not the same as being able to feel another person's hardship as though it were happening to us.

Traditionally, empathy may have been relegated to personal interactions, but in today's world, we experience business and the personal as intertwined and holistic. Think of empathy as a muscle that can be developed. Once developed, it can be used throughout your life. We often think of it as a quality that helps us in our personal relationships. But an unfortunate error so many make is to think of the business world as a place of facts, figures, features, and benefits. The principles of empathy are transportable into the business and corporate realm. Business empathy is the ability to perceive a client's unmet needs. For us, business empathy is about understanding not what we have to offer, but what our clients need and want. It sounds simple, but it is not common. Empathy may be the greatest professional skill we possess.

We believe that empathy is one of the most neglected subjects in business and culture today, even as it has become a more important multidisciplinary concern. It may be a challenging skill to hone, but possessing empathy helps us serve others in powerful ways and can be the key differentiator between commoditized services and sought-after skills valued for their relevance. Empathy helps us understand the challenges of others on a personal level; it can also help us put ourselves into the shoes of the clients and customers we serve, so that our service can be improved. We live without empathy at our peril, and also risk missing the gifts with which empathy enriches our lives. If empathy is a luxury, it is a luxury we can't afford to do without.

We'd be hard-pressed to identify an author who shaped a more empathetic character than Harper Lee when she created Atticus Finch, the quiet country lawyer said to be based on her father. In *To Kill a Mockingbird*, Lee galvanized readers with Finch's integrity in defense of an African-American man. Reading it again in this new millennium, we are also struck by the deep empathy Lee summons for the loathsome Bob Ewell. Even after Ewell framed Finch's client for rape and spit in Finch's face, Lee vividly paints Finch's empathy for Ewell: "Atticus didn't bat an eye, just took out his handkerchief and wiped his face and stood there and let Mr. Ewell call him names."

Lee shows us that Finch was a master of his craft in the courtroom. Her character quietly created for the jury a picture of the Ewells' brutal home life. Finch questioned Ewell with clarity and focus—with mastery—eliciting the facts he needed to make his case. His questions exposed Ewell's story for the lie it was.

When Ewell responds with frustrated anger on the stand, Harper Lee has Finch do something extraordinary. She shows the reader how mastery can be married to empathy. Rather than reacting to Ewell's fury with contempt or reciprocal antagonism, Finch stands silent. We are given a vivid image of a man whose actions are guided by his understanding of Ewell's character. Without the insight to comprehend that the Ewells of this world lash out when they are challenged, this story might have taken a very different direction. Instead, we see that Finch relies on his perception to guide his response, enabling him not only to deliver a legal defense, but also to intuit the danger Ewell poses to others, and to deflect it as best he can.

Afterward, Lee's explanation of Ewell's behavior captures the essence of empathy. "Jem," Finch tells his young son, "see if you can stand in Bob Ewell's shoes a minute. I destroyed his last shred of credibility at that trial, if he had any to begin with. The man had to have some kind of comeback, his kind always does. So if spitting in my face and threatening me saved Mayella Ewell one extra beating, that's something I'll gladly take." By assessing the situation with compassionate as well as professional gifts, Lee's Finch models empathy in a way that becomes an inspiration. The timeless significance of Harper Lee's message imbues her novel with the power of a touchstone, keeping us grounded to what is right and true.

THE RISE OF NARCISSISM. THE FALL OF EMPATHY.

That touchstone may never be more critical than it is today. Social psychologist Sara Konrath analyzed the results of 72 studies that administered the Davis Interpersonal Reactivity Index (IRI) questionnaire to college students between 1979 and 2009. The IRI is considered the gold standard for measuring an individual's capacity for empathy. Konrath found that the empathy scores of tested college students are about 40 percent lower than the scores of students 20 years ago. The decline in empathy has been particularly steep since 2000. Concurrently, scores measuring narcissism are on the rise.

We don't have hard data identifying the causes behind flagging empathy and rising narcissism, but some recent cultural trends are being eyed with concern. Burgeoning options for electronic communication enable us to interact with a multitude of people in online social networks, but may be creating a distance that diminishes our interpersonal skills and buffers us from the painful emotions that force us to confront our shortcomings on the journey of personal growth. When individuals break off relationships via a text or by changing their Facebook status, they never have to confront the pain in their partner's eyes. Challenging economic times have influenced people entering the job market to delay marriage and families. Arguably, this delays the experience of obligation, responsibility, and awareness of community that confronts new parents.

Narcissism and commoditization are rising hand in hand. As we work with clients around the globe, we see them struggling to establish distinction for products, services, and business solutions that are being commoditized across business segments, industries, countries, and cultures. The creep of commoditization continues, and it is extending beyond products to people. Garment workers and IT professionals are being replaced by less expensive counterparts in other countries. It's hard to imagine an experience more personally devaluing than being replaced by a less expensive version of ourselves.

THE MORE YOU THINK OF YOURSELF, THE LESS YOU MATTER.

How we show up in the world matters; in fact, how we show up is our only sustainable distinguisher in a commoditized world. Being empathetic gives us a natural advantage; it allows us to be relevantly engaged in ways that narcissists can never be.

Narcissism is a self-penalizing approach to life. A narcissistic person never entertains a perspective beyond himself; he never leaves his shoes. True empathy requires us to slide out of our own shoes and feel what it is like to be in the shoes of another person.

One of Phil's partner organizations in London, Consalia, conducted some interesting research with the London School of Economics. They interviewed more than 154 key decision makers across cultures and business sectors, and asked a simple question: Of the suppliers and sales professionals that you see, what percentage of them are business relevant?

When the study was initiated, Phil knew the percentage would be small, but he was still stunned by the results. Decision makers reported that only 7 percent, or less than one out of 10 salespeople, were perceived as business relevant. As one respondent observed: "Most of the salespeople that we encounter are human brochures. They come in walking and talking about their own company's features and benefits."

Listening actively is much more difficult than presenting a preformulated solution. But when we are focused on our own solution, we develop a tunnel vision that's not necessarily good for our clients. When test subjects are directed to notice the white things in a room and then to close their eyes, their memory is good—for white objects. But when they are asked to name a single green object in the room, they can't think of anything. In their concentration on what was white, they were unable to see anything else. In business, we dub that "product glaucoma." In our personal and our professional lives, we often only see only what matters to us. This is a form of "emotional glaucoma," and it does not cultivate relevance. The more we can train ourselves to see the entire landscape, the more we will notice, the more helpful we can be to others, and the more relevant we become.

Consalia pushed further, to find out what distinguished the people perceived as relevant. They discovered that the number-one distinguisher of relevant salespeople was that they are able to look beyond their own products and services, and provide industry insights based on their observations working with other companies in the same field. Decision makers wanted to know what was working for other companies. This requires the observational skills to analyze an industry, and the empathy to identify promising methodologies and strategies. It is a skill that may strike us as obvious, but it is not common.

Phil incorporated these research insights into his company's sales training with a program simulating 15-minute business conversations guided by case studies. Participants role-play with fictitious customers to hone the relationship-building skills that generate relevance. Over the last two to three years, Phil's trainers have noticed a higher incidence of participants who freeze at the five-minute mark while attempting to sustain these conversations. When queried, the stymied participants explained that they didn't know where to go next with the conversation. They struggled with the empathetic interpersonal skills to transcend their own perspective and move into conversations focused on their clients' interests.

STEPPING OUT OF THE SPOTLIGHT
TO MAKE ROOM FOR OTHERS.

In response, Phil's team has developed a training technique that uses what are called "careabouts." The careabouts tool refocuses attention from self to others, and teaches salespeople to focus on learning about potential customer careabouts. Participants learn that we don't connect to others by focusing on our own concerns or products; it is only by developing our sense of what our client cares about that we become relevant to them. A bottle of water sitting in our car has no value to us—until we find that we are thirsty and care about quenching our thirst. This may sound simplistic, but for some people, the careabout notion is an epiphany. We believe that understanding careabouts is a basic rule of selling, and of life. We can't be relevant unless we understand the careabouts of others.

EMPATHY IS THE FOUNDATION
OF SERVING OTHERS.

How we show up as authentic, empathetic human beings is what creates a sense of connection with others—and connection is impervious to commoditization. Our deep interest in empathy is rooted in our belief that we are here on this planet to serve others and to have a positive impact on them. We can't make an impact unless what we are offering is perceived as meeting someone's needs. Being relevant gives us the ability to make an impact and to ultimately serve others. It is that service that is a marker of a life that matters more. Relevance is the fuel cell of the significance that we bring to our life, and empathy provides the docking station that enables us to connect with others. Our concept of service is about mattering more to others; but more importantly, it is about mattering more for others.

Incorporating the acumen of empathy in our personal and business lives requires us to make a shift from self-absorption to self-donation. Until we realize life isn't exclusively about us, we are not going to be able to understand others well enough to make sense of their needs. Living our lives from a sense of genuine interest to understand what others care about distinguishes us in a very sustainable way. Empathy enables us to see the world through another person's viewpoint, and to understand how another's feelings color their perception and drive their needs. When we approach a problem from another's perspective as well as from our own, we can better employ our gifts to creatively address needs, provide support, and build a sense of trust that strengthens all of our relationships.

Empathetic people listen attentively; they donate their complete attention to the person in front of them. They focus, and they spend more time listening than talking because they want to understand. Understanding with empathy expands our grasp of the issues at stake. When we practice these attributes, we make those around us feel heard and acknowledged.

THREE LEVELS OF EMPATHY.

As individuals in relationships, we have always yearned for understanding; and we value those who make us feel seen. As professionals and businesses in a rapidly changing marketplace, we recognize that the ironclad guarantees of experts and gurus no longer serve uncertain economic environments. "Fail fast" nimble adaptation is the new key to survival. Shifting environments have introduced a new sense of vulnerability into our world, and empathy serves vulnerability with a responsiveness that the hard-and-fast wisdom of the past cannot offer. Today, a business approach that acknowledges vulnerability resonates. When we open with empathy and vulnerability, we are reassuring our clients that we are open to figuring out, with them, the tools they need to accomplish their objectives, instead of trying to force our favorite tool on them whether they need it or not.

In our relationships and our work, we have observed that empathy can operate on three distinct levels. Empathy's value is real at each level, but the perception of another's needs must be much keener to operate at the highest level than it needs to be at the first level. The three levels of empathic response are reactive empathy, solution-based empathy, and transcendent empathy.

Reactive empathy. This is ground-floor empathy. Someone asks for something, and we give it to him or her. This is not inspired empathy, but it's perfectly adequate, and there are situations where this is the type of empathy that's needed. A car company's "cup holder survey" is an apt example of on-demand empathy. When an automotive company questions how many cup holders to offer in their cars, they can frankly ask their prospective customers how many cup holders they would like. They send out a cup-holder survey and tally the results. People ask for six cup holders, so that is the number of cup holders designed into the vehicles.

Solution-based empathy. Solution-based empathy begins with a specific demand, but then generates an enhanced solution. This is empathy that looks beyond satisfying a direct request, to create a more imaginative win-win solution. When Amazon customers complained about the cost of shipping on their Amazon orders, and asked for a shipping cost reduction, Amazon looked beyond simply satisfying the demand to lower shipping fees. Their solution? Rather than lowering the fees, Amazon created Amazon Prime, a program offering unlimited shipping for a single annual fee. They created a win-win, even though their solution was not exactly what the consumer asked for.

Transcendent empathy. Both on-demand and solution-based empathy generate solutions in response to specific requests. Transcendent empathy is different; it creates a solution for a problem that hasn't even been articulated. The type of reflection that addresses unidentified needs requires us to think on a much higher level about people's wants and preferences. Jonathan Ive, the industrial designer credited with designing many of Apple's most innovative products, reflected transcendent empathy when he explained that Apple was engaged in solving problems that people don't even know they have.

Apple deliberately employs transcendent empathy in the design of their products, searching for the most beautiful fonts, the most intuitive graphical interface, and the most appealing design. Much has been written about Steve Jobs and the clarity with which he defined and pursued his mission. He captured the essence of transcendent empathy when he observed: "You can't just ask customers what they want and then try to give that to them. By the time you get it built, they'll want something new." But the path to transcendent solutions is not always a deliberately and consciously charted course.

One of our favorite examples of transcendent problem solving, accomplished by a company headquartered in our home state of Minnesota, was not deliberate at all. The essential office product used by almost everyone, the Post-it Note®, began as a failure in the 3M research laboratories. In 1970, chemist Spencer Silver was trying to develop a superglue for 3M. His work resulted in the opposite of what he'd intended. Instead of making a stronger adhesive, he'd created a weaker, pressure-sensitive, low-tack adhesive that could easily be removed after it had been attached, without leaving marks or residue. Silver had no idea how his adhesive could be used, but something prompted him to hold on to his temporary glue. Four years later, another 3M scientist—and church choir member—thought of Silver's glue when he was looking for a way to anchor page markers in his hymnbook. He coated his markers with Silver's adhesive. They stuck without damaging the hymnal pages.

Intrigued, 3M invested in the development of moveable paper markers coated with Silver's glue. When Tom's friend Sue Wasserman was assigned to market 3M's Post-it Note program, she distributed free samples of the markers to a test market of executive secretaries in Boise, Idaho. Instead of approaching purchasing agents about the notes, 3M invited the end users to explore the stickable, movable notes for themselves. The exercise helped 3M to see the markers through the eyes of their customers. In effect, 3M asked, "Standing in your own shoes, would you like to use our notes?" By standing in the shoes of their customers, 3M came to realize the potential of their quirky glue. When the trial concluded, 90 percent of the trial participants said that they would buy the sticky markers—and wanted to keep the ones they had.

No one had asked for a sticky note that could be positioned and repositioned in all sorts of different places. No one set out to create a weak adhesive that would allow us to position and then reposition markers. But curiosity and a sense of possibility prompted 3M scientists not to discard their odd, weak adhesive. Today, we write on Post-It Notes, we use them to mark our place, we put them down, then we pick them up and reposition them at will. Post-it Notes, a product no one had requested or even imagined, have become essential in the arsenal of office supplies.

EMPATHY AND HAPPINESS.

The power of empathy to deepen understanding and increase the value of our service is compelling motivation to develop our empathetic capacity. But the rewards of empathy may be broader. Psychology suggests that empathy and happiness are closely related in a dance that rewards us with a host of benefits. Harvard Medical School has published a Special Health Report on the importance of positive psychology, noting that we achieve satisfaction through being engaged, doing good, and focusing on the present. The techniques that strengthen empathy in our business and personal relationships can help us improve the degree of "flow" we feel when we are engaged in projects. They increase our resilience, maximize concentration, and enable us to more fully savor life's pleasures. In short, the links between empathy, happiness, and productive success suggest that increased relevance may be only one of a plethora of empathy's rewards.

EMPATHY FOR THE BIRDS.

From April to November, Tom loves to read out on his screened-in porch, surrounded by the sounds of nature: frogs, crickets, birds, and the occasional jumping fish. While most of nature's ambience couldn't be more pleasant, in late summer, an especially grating sound can be heard. Imagine a prolonged call that combines the squeal of a creaking door, fingernails across a chalkboard, and the screeching of monstrous creatures in a horror movie.

Knowing his birds, Tom guessed that he was hearing some sort of raptor, perhaps a screech owl or a nighthawk. But an Internet search revealed that the calls of those birds were infinitely more pleasant than this call. Further searches proved futile. Week after week, the screeching persisted and Tom's annoyance grew. This irritating mystery pest was ruining his pleasant sanctuary.

A few weeks later, while out on an early-morning walk, Tom heard the noise again. In the predawn light, he spotted the culprit bird in a tree, screeching away. As his feathered nemesis became visible in the dawn light, Tom saw that it was indeed an owl, similar in appearance to a great horned owl, but smaller.

A few minutes later, an actual great horned owl flew up with some sort of meat, and fed it to the screeching bird. The screeching stopped.

Tom realized that the screech was owned by a juvenile great horned owl, calling for food. This new understanding not only solved a mystery, it also completely changed the way Tom came to view the screech. It was no longer an obnoxious noise uttered for the sole purpose of disturbing Tom's peace. Now Tom understood that he was hearing a hungry young bird calling to a parent for food. While the sound of the call would never be pleasant, it lost its harsh edge and became another of the wonderful night sounds of nature surrounding Tom as he reads on summer evenings.

That is the power of empathy. When we understand needs, we come to understand behaviors in a whole new light. If we are lucky, we can apply our strengths to meeting those needs and to creating happiness for both the recipients and ourselves.

THE DYNAMICS OF EMPATHY
AND HAPPINESS IN THE WORKPLACE.

Most individuals, and companies, follow a motivational formula for building success through an emphasis on the qualities of mastery. They reason that if they work harder at developing their talents, they will be more successful, and that the success they win will deliver satisfaction and relevance. Unfortunately, an approach to success based exclusively on mastery does not work.

When we make happiness and satisfaction dependent on application of our skills to attain a goal, we are focusing our attention on the space between our present and the future success to which we aspire. We anticipate that the achievement of our goal will be rewarded with the happiness we seek. However, the "achievement will yield happiness" approach doesn't deliver happiness. Instead, every victory creates a new achievement to strive for, and inches the happiness reward a bit further out of reach. We achieved our sales goal? We won't be rewarded with the luxury of resting on our laurels—instead, we'll get a new sales goal that will be a bit higher than the last one. Scored a prestigious promotion? Chances are that as we settle into our new office, we are already thinking about how to improve our skills to win the title one step further up the ladder. When we operate out of the belief that achievement rewards us with happiness, we lose sight of the fact that there is always one more success to win. We progress continually toward that next moving target goal, and the golden ring of happiness moves along with our aspirations, always just out of reach.

POSITIVELY BETTER.

This motivational formula bars us from what positive psychologists call the "happiness advantage." In order to experience this happiness advantage, we have to change the model in a way that raises our level of positive satisfaction and optimism in the present—instead of delaying happiness or allowing some

STYRLUND & HAYES *with* DEEGAN

future success to hold it hostage. When we pursue goals in a state of happy optimism in the present, research suggests that our productivity is significantly improved. Optimism releases dopamine into the brain. Dopamine not only makes us happier, it also activates the brain's learning centers. Happy people perform significantly better than people who are stressed. Creativity, productivity, and energy levels rise. We become better at securing and keeping jobs. We are more resilient, experiencing less burnout and less turnover. When we feel positive, we work harder and more intelligently. However, when we make happiness the reward of future success, we don't allow ourselves to experience happiness in the present, and we deny ourselves all of the productive advantages happiness provides.

Positive emotions support our capacity for empathy and increase our mastery by encouraging creation and exploration. In contrast, negative emotions prompt guarded, survival-oriented behaviors. The interplay between positive emotion and empathy is being explored in three areas that influence the dynamics of relevance, and the research findings are fascinating:

- **Happiness optimizes our experience of the relationships and interests that are part of healthy living.**

- **Confident absorption in our work fosters the experience of immersion, or "flow," as we practice our signature skills, increasing our productivity.**

- **When we employ empathy to contribute to an aspect of life that feels larger than ourselves, we experience a positive sense of meaning and purpose.**

When we cultivate optimism in the present moment, we are more likely to take the time to connect with others, increasing the interactions that enable us to understand their fears, needs, wants, joys, what makes them tick, and what gets them ticked. By cultivating and approaching our lives with conscious empathy, we create a docking station that allows us to match our gifts to others' needs. Without empathy, this connection doesn't happen.

HOW DO WE DEVELOP EMPATHY?

We are familiar with the personality typing tools that help us dig down to our authenticity and identify our signature strengths, the discipline and practice mastery requires, and the plans, strategies, and tactics that funnel understanding and skill into action. Developing empathy is a more subtle, but no less important, art in the relevance equation. Empathy is also more challenging to achieve in the throes of the modern world's fears of commoditization. When we feel threatened and afraid, it is tough to be open to understanding another perspective by stepping into someone else's shoes. In the face of uncertainty, we focus on looking out for ourselves. Our willingness to extend empathy declines. The temptation is to stay in our fortress and bar the door.

Can empathy be taught or cultivated? This is a tantalizing question without a sure answer. We have discovered guidelines that have been helpful for us.

THE THREE METACOMPONENTS OF EMPATHY.

Be a student of humankind.

In the pages of the books that expand our perspective, and in our curiosity about the lives of people around us, we discover similarities that connect us. In the stories of friends and colleagues and chance strangers well met, we discover familiar experiences and kindred observations that confirm our own experiences. In their stories, we may also be introduced to perspectives very different from our own, approaches that inspire us to reconsider our own assumptions about human nature.

Empathy begins with understanding, and understanding begins with curiosity. When we are open to input, we are in a better position to learn. Empathy's challenge is to approach understanding without preconceived notions. This is easier said than done. We all operate within assumptions about the way the world works, some of them deeply ingrained. People with a deep belief in original sin tend to find that people are sinful. People who believe in the indomitable human spirit tend to identify courage in those around them. Our goal is to open our posture to possibilities, and then to evoke the practice of empathy: listening. Success requires practice; we exercise empathy the same way that we would exercise any muscle. The empathetic listener avails herself of the data presented to her, and does her best to avoid projecting her own views. When she listens, she tries to focus on understanding needs instead of on reacting to what is said. Only when she understands needs can she get past the noise and down to what is really going on.

Although J. R. R. Tolkien lived a relatively quiet professorial life in the company of a small circle of friends, his empathy for the human condition was masterful. He left England only twice, once to hike in Switzerland as a young man, and again as an ambulance driver in World War I. Yet his masterpiece, *The Lord of the Rings*, reveals impressive insight into human nature. He understands our temptations, with great compassion for the nuanced manifestations of good and evil in the human heart. His introverted ways did not prevent him from acquiring an intimate knowledge of what makes people tick. Certainly he and his close circle of friends were among the most well-read people of his century, conducting robust intellectual discussions. As Tolkien demonstrates, we don't have to be extroverts or globetrotting adventurers to inform empathy. There are many paths to understanding.

Desire to be of service.

Once we recognize our own humanity though authenticity, we can turn a more compassionate eye to those around us. We can explore our communities as students of humankind and cultivate a passion to learn about what motivates others. This sounds really simple. And yet, as marketers and coaches, we see our share of people who struggle to see beyond their own needs, even when they are convinced that they are as empathetic as anyone. We can spot these folks in a meeting. They don't engage their listeners, their presentations are canned, and their pitches feel formatted. They are the walking brochures.

When we concentrate on our own priorities, without considering them in the context of our listener's concerns and needs, we remain in our own world, and our chances of resonating with our listener's needs are slim. Only empathy can actively engage the interest of the listener, building a bridge that can take us to the heart of connection.

Know how to listen.

Caring means cultivating the skills of an active listener. That is easier said than done, as an anecdote about the extraordinary social skills of British politician Benjamin Disraeli and his rival William Gladstone illustrates. A warm friend to many, including Queen Victoria, Disraeli was seen as a shrewd statesman, man of letters, and Byronic hero by his admirers. Four-time Prime Minister Gladstone was famous for his commitment to electoral reform, conservative public spending, and passionate oratory.

The rivalry between the two statesmen piqued the curiosity of American Jennie Jerome, admired beauty and the mother of Winston Churchill. Ms. Jerome arranged to dine with Gladstone and then with Disraeli, on consecutive evenings. Afterward, she described the difference between the two men this way: "When I left the dining room after sitting next to Gladstone, I thought he was the cleverest man in England. But when I sat next to Disraeli, I left feeling that I was the cleverest woman."

For whom would we prefer to carve out time in our calendar? The person who impresses us with his intelligence or the person who appreciates and applauds our own gifts?

Good listeners step back from their own concerns and into the role of detective, actively listening to the words of their companions, with attention to figuring out what it is they are proud of, interested in, fearful of, or angry about. Even when an idea sounds peculiar, adept listeners look for some benefit in the information being presented. By cultivating openness, great listeners learn about the things that are important to others. When we employ our understanding of humankind and adopt a posture that avails itself to understanding an individual's needs, people respond. An empathetic bond is formed, and everyone benefits.

THE TOOLS OF EMPATHY.

Moving beyond a focus on self to think of others and connect with them is a skill. Exercising this skill requires knowledge of people, a sincere motivation to care, and the ability to employ our mastery in service to them. These are the basics, the metaskills. Over the years, we have discovered and explored tools to help us strengthen these metaskills. We use these tools both to create connection and to evaluate whether our skills can address and add value to our clients' needs.

Empathy informs our assessment of a given situation, to help us determine whether our skills can serve others in a meaningful way. Unless mastery and empathy go hand in hand, we can't be sure that the talents we offer are actually needed by those to whom we offer them. If our skills aren't helpful to those we serve, relevance will remain beyond our grasp.

HUMOR.

Experiencing life's victories and failures provides us with the context to understand the emotions of others going through similar experiences. Our failures are valuable lessons. They can teach us humility, and tolerance for our limitations and for the limitations of others. If we were always successful, how could we accept our own faults, let alone cultivate an understanding of the faults of others? Failure teaches us empathetic understanding. When we communicate our understanding through humor, shared laughter transforms the ordinary into a shared sense of appreciative intimacy. It fosters close interpersonal relationships. For those of us on the journey to deepen empathy, humor is a valuable tool to establish connection and build relationships.

THESE SHOES AREN'T MADE FOR WALKING.

Tom and one of his closest friends go back almost 40 years. They met in the Boy Scouts—hiking, canoeing, playing capture the flag, and crawling in caves. Together, they've seen babies born, parents buried, and children married. They still hike along rocky shorelines and take their own adult children to the Boundary Waters. Tom's friend has achieved remarkable accomplishments. He's become a lawyer, run a foundation, served as president of a college board, raised two great kids, and contributed his considerable skills to numerous good causes. He is articulate, witty, and a skilled conversationalist equally at home at small dinner parties and in large groups.

But there is something about him that makes strangers feel awkward and self-conscious—it's his wheelchair. When he senses that people are uncomfortable, he has this wonderful shtick. He grabs his leg and pulls it up so it crosses his knee. He points to his foot and starts going on about his wonderful shoes. He'll exclaim: "I've had these shoes for more than a decade. And look at that tread—it hasn't worn a bit. Boy, they don't make shoes like these anymore." Invariably the strangers nod in approval and agreement. Then suddenly they realize that he wasn't just pulling up his own leg, he was pulling theirs—people who don't walk, don't wear out their shoes! In the end, it's just Tom's friend's way of saying, "I also noticed that I am in a wheelchair and it's OK."

This joke is a stroke of empathetic genius, and understanding why it's funny can teach us a lot about the power of empathic awareness. First, we often find humor in things that make us uncomfortable—like people who are different from us. Second, the sly self-deprecation breaks the tension and lets people off the hook for feeling awkward. Finally, we all take delight in moments of psychological closure, and Tom's friend has found a gentle and nonthreatening way to guide folks through their discomposure. Those who don't know people in wheelchairs have trouble comprehending the ramifications of not being able to walk. They don't always grasp that in a wheelchair, you get lots of years, but not any miles, out of your shoes. These people are, literally, unable to put themselves in Tom's friend's shoes. But when they get the joke, they can. Tom's friend takes it upon himself to use his wit to gently and kindly invite people to sit down with him at empathy's table.

FUELED CURIOSITY.

Intellectual appetite is a definite advantage when we want to draw others out. Some of us are naturally curious; we'll sit down with anyone, eager to hear stories and experience the human spirit from a new or different perspective. Those of us who aren't quite so extroverted can still benefit from behaving like a curious person. People value the ability to provide insights.

We can feed our curiosity, as well as the curiosity of those around us, by keeping in mind the three currencies of relationships:

- **Insights**—how does a particular problem fit into a larger context? How might someone else have solved this issue? That's insight.

- **Hindsights**—what has life taught us, and what reflections might we bring to bear on the problem at hand? What lessons do we have to offer?

- **Foresights**—what might matter next in the context of the issue on the table? What challenges are on the horizon, and how might our actions now affect our future?

The next time we are preparing for a meeting, we can try using the currencies of relationships to jot down three to five questions to include in our conversation. Chances are that we will learn more. Over time, the act of creating questions becomes habitual. Before we know it, we won't just behave like a curious person—we'll actually be more curious in our interactions.

George Washington Carver's legacy exemplifies the power of empathetic curiosity. He developed more than 100 recipes for the humble peanut, but his curiosity didn't stop there. Inspired to discover innovative uses for this ordinary crop, Carver's research resulted in the use of the peanut in products as diverse as paints, dyes, cosmetics, plastics, and nitroglycerin. This scientist, botanist, and inventor observed: "Anything will give up its secrets if you love it enough. Not only have I found that when I talk to the little flower or to the little peanut, they will give up their secrets, but I have found that when I … commune with people, they give up their secrets also—if you love them enough."

NURTURE TOLERANCE.

The practice of empathy requires us to draw on inner resources and extend support with active attentiveness. This takes energy. We have to be in a good place. Assessing our capacity for empathy means monitoring our tolerance budget on a regular basis. When we are dealing with a job loss or a death in the family or a stressful relationship, we have less energy available to give to others, less tolerance for others' demands. When we are mentally, emotionally, physically depleted, we have nothing to give away. We encourage purpose-driven selfishness, because we understand that we have to care for ourselves in order to serve others. As flight attendants instruct us, when the oxygen masks drop, we are to put on our own mask first before we help others with theirs. This is not selfishness; it's emotional pragmatism.

We must satisfy the basics of physiological survival and address our basic needs for security and safety before we can turn our attention to higher-level needs like friendship and respect of others. It is appropriate to first conserve our own resources and nurture our own healthy function. Once our reserve needs are met, we can extend our resources in empathy.

DEPENDABLE RITUAL.

Phil thrives on international travel. By visiting regularly with clients in intercontinental locations from London to Dubai, he is constantly gathering information from the businesses he serves. His conversations with clients help him to hone market insights and identify global trends as they emerge. On any given day, it is a challenge to predict which time zone his schedule has arranged for him. And yet, his friends, associates, and clients always know exactly where he is. Each morning without fail, Phil records a fresh greeting on his voice mail, identifying his location for the day. In the midst of his globetrotting, this habit, which Phil calls one of his dependable rituals, has built a valuable perception of Phil's trustworthiness throughout his circles.

We have found that seemingly small acts like Phil's, performed with consistency, can create a sense of reliability in an uncertain world. Just as there are tools to maintain our own reserves, dependable ritual is a tool we can use to create and maintain a sense of trustworthiness with others. Personal empathy involves a one-on-one relationship between two people. Professional empathy projects a commitment to understanding and service based on sensitivity to customer or client needs. Both dynamics engender trust. A personal or professional brand that is perceived as trustworthy will enhance the confidence that is the currency of empathy.

Phil's dependable rituals do exactly that, acting as touchstones for his entire circle of friends and professional contacts. We have come to think of dependable rituals as a component of our personal promise of authenticity: they are the rituals that demonstrate, sometimes in subtle yet powerful ways, the qualities that contribute to our unique relevance.

Phil created his dependable rituals by challenging himself to come up with three personal practices that represented parts of his authentic self. He understood that especially in an unpredictable world, when uncertainty is the new normal, we long for dependability and are attracted to anyone or anything that demonstrates consistent trustworthiness. Dependable rituals are so compelling because they are not merely the flags of our personal brand; they are also acts of empathy, a reassurance in response to the "in your shoes" understanding that all of us are hungry for dependability.

People can deal with almost anything when they know they are not alone. Phil's voice message can't solve anyone's issues, but it communicates an ineffable but powerful reassurance. Phil's colleagues may not reach him every time they call, but the reassurance, through his voice mail update, that they could reach him satisfies a need for connection that we all feel. Communicating to others that they are not alone is a potent tool in building relevance. How often have we heard people speak longingly of the days when customer service issues were solved by talking with "a real person"? We may not be able to solve all of the problems brought to our door, but we can develop our own set of authentic rituals to reassure our community of contacts that they are not alone as they work through life's challenges.

TRANSCENDING THE NEED TO BE RIGHT.

Before we can effectively put our talents to work in a meaningful way for others, it is wise to check in with our assumptions about the value of our own abilities. Our conscious self is strongly attached to self-serving biases. We are fairly good at accurately estimating the skills of others, but we persistently overestimate our own abilities. In order for our gifts to be perceived as relevant, we have to see them accurately, so that we can understand when they are appropriate to address the needs of others.

How do we work our way past our self-serving biases? Finding fault in our own behavior is uncomfortable, but when we acknowledge our missteps, we engender the power to take responsibility for our own actions, and create the awareness to do better next time. The tools we use to hone mastery serve us equally well in developing empathy: we improve when we review our own performance for errors, learn from our mistakes, and correct them.

Related to our tendency to overestimate our own value is the compulsion to be right in any given situation. We all have an inner voice that offers opinionated commentary about information we encounter. It is easy to fall into the trap of focusing our attention on that inner voice. Our inner voice prevents us from listening openly to opinions that are contrary to our own, and may even cause us to tune out before we understand the entire premise of a situation. It is a fascinating exercise to tune down our inner voice and realign our sympathies with the speaker. We may be surprised at what we hear. Every time the inner voice contradicts an opinion, try pausing to suggest all the reasons why the inner voice may be wrong and another perspective may be right. This can help us open ourselves to the information being provided, and have powerful consequences.

Once we disengage from the impulse to prove our point, we don't have to be worried about critiquing or fixing. We can focus our attention on caring about the speaker's point of view. Phil remembers his father teaching this approach during family vacations.

"As we travel the world, there are many ways to live life," he would say. "They aren't right or wrong. Think of these unfamiliar ways as different instead of wrong. Just insert the word 'different.'" When Phil and his siblings followed their dad's advice, it opened the opportunity to consider other possibilities and engaged their curiosity about the varying viewpoints of the people they met.

THE DISCIPLINE TO PAUSE.

One of the keys to the practice of empathy is to rein in the urge to leap to a solution. We should pause to be sure we understand the question before we start formulating answers. When Amazon clients asked for lower shipping costs, Amazon did not jump to a literal face-value solution. The organization paused to consider both the motivation for their customers' shipping fee concerns and the effect of adjusted shipping fees on their business model.

Thoughtful, empathetic consideration enabled the company to create an incentive solution that benefited everyone.

Pausing can also help us to identify the situations where there is not a match between our skills and what others need. In those situations, it is better to bow out and suggest a better fit than to take on a task that we are not equipped to handle effectively. Pausing helps us to develop what Jack Fortin, author of *The Centered Life*, describes as a truly non-anxious presence. It helps us to practice empathy with wisdom, and guides us to balance others' needs against our talents. As a result, we are better able to avoid the mistakes of pressing unneeded skills on clients, or taking on projects that require skills beyond our repertoire.

THE RULE OF FIVE WHYS.

Originally developed by Sakichi Toyoda and used to develop manufacturing methodologies within Toyota Motor Corporation, this question-asking technique is useful in clarifying both the nature of a problem and its solution. The concept is as simple as it sounds. We ask the question "Why?" five times. What this repetition will do is unbundle the issue and allow us to get to the higher-order issue. We describe the dynamics of this tool using the metaphor of Russian nesting dolls. Every time we ask why, we are opening a deeper level of the problem to further examination. As we continue to probe, we move further toward the core of the issue and uncover a table full of dolls—or facets of the problem—that were not evident at first glance.

This Five Whys tool is a powerful empathy builder that has been adapted to widespread use beyond manufacturing, with applications as varied as Six Sigma training, improving sales effectiveness, and as a psychological motivation technique.

The value of the rule of Five Whys lies in its power to feed curiosity and to set aside our own thoughts and assumptions so that we can more clearly see a situation from someone else's perspective. Many of us might not analyze a situation beyond asking ourselves what we would do in that situation—which doesn't tell us much about the view from someone else's shoes. Exploring a problem by probing the proffered explanation with a succession of "whys" helps us to avoid assumptions and instead encourage our partner to trace the chain of causality.

This same technique can be a powerful tool in business. Phil uses the Five Whys technique in his sales training. In one exercise designed to prepare a client going into a large deal, the client team undergoes a two-day analysis called "red team/blue team." The team is split; one team role-plays the organization's role in the deal, and the other team takes the posture of their competitor. By literally putting his client into their competitor's shoes, Phil is able to teach them structured business empathy from their competition's viewpoint. As a part of this training, Phil employs the rule of Five Whys to teach people to understand not only the nature of the needs of the parties, but also the underlying dynamics driving those needs. The brilliance of this tool is that salespeople—just like the rest of us—may not be able to remember 30 questions. But we can all remember "why." And "why" works. We don't have to have it all figured out; we just have to keep digging. Why provides our customer or client or friend with the opportunity to tell us what they need, to put us into their shoes.

THE PLATINUM RULE: ADDING MORE VALUE TO THE GOLDEN RULE.

We learned the Golden Rule as children: Do unto others as you would have them do unto you. This rule assumes that other people want to be treated the way we want to be treated. As valuable as this rule can be, when we apply a shallow interpretation to it and take it to mean that we should apply our motivations and desires to another's situation, we can find ourselves in trouble.

Phil learned the problem with misapplying the Golden Rule the hard way. He was the head of sales at ADC Telecommunications, and his assistant's name was Kelly. She was extraordinary at her job, and the linchpin of the sales organization. She worked with Phil to organize an extremely successful program for almost 700 salespeople, and Phil wanted to do something special to recognize her stellar work. He commissioned a plaque, and at the close of the program, he made an announcement.

"Before we wrap up," he said, "I want to acknowledge the person who is really the heart and soul of this place. Kelly, please join me on the stage." With Kelly standing beside him, Phil spoke at length about the greatness of Kelly, showering her with accolades. Afterward, Kelly sought Phil out. She was fuming. "If you ever do that to me again," she told Phil, "I will quit. Being in front of an audience like that—that is my worst fear."

Phil realized, too late, that he had recognized Kelly in the way that would have meant the most to him—not to her. If he had approached the situation from Kelly's perspective, he would have recalled that Kelly loved small county fairs and fine dining. With the clarity of hindsight, Phil understood that Kelly would probably have been delighted to be taken out to lunch and given Friday off with a gift certificate to her favorite restaurant.

Most of us are guilty of putting other people in our shoes, with our preferences, wants, and needs—at one time or another—just as Phil did. We plan a huge celebration to surprise our spouse on an important birthday, without considering that although we would love an extroverted bash for our hundred favorite people, our introverted partner might prefer a quiet dinner with just a few dear friends. We make dinner reservations at our favorite seafood restaurant, forgetting that one of our colleagues is allergic to shellfish. Businesses compensate employees in what management deems to be really important and valuable ways, when it turns out that the employees' definition of important and valuable is something else entirely. There are few things more disconcerting than discovering that the nice thing you were trying to do made people angry, instead of delighted.

It all comes back to the shoes. When you are standing in your own shoes, you are convinced that your view of the world is beyond dispute—and it is, but only within the frame of your own perspective. The result? "Interpersonal glaucoma" or false empathy: the inability to see some things because we are looking through our own lens. What feels like empathy to us is in fact empathy for our own view, and that is not actually empathy. As long as we stay in our own shoes, we are stuck. We can't transcend our own perspective until we kick off our own shoes and step into someone else's.

If an oversimplified application of the Golden Rule puts us at risk for developing interpersonal glaucoma, what is the alternative? There is another way to think about the Golden Rule: the Platinum Rule, which advises us to treat others the way they would like to be treated.

The difference in perspective can be huge. The Platinum Rule shifts our focus from "I'll give people what I want" to "I'll take the time to understand what other people want, and I'll give them what they would like to receive." This change in focus helps us to recognize that what makes our friends or colleagues happy can be utterly different from what would make us happy. It is the mindset that looks—and asks—for a way to add value. It empowers us to sit down and ask, "What can I do to help you today?" and then listen to someone explain what is important to him or her.

Phil has seen the Platinum Rule applied with enormous success by one of his clients. Every year, this organization recognized its top sales performers with a generous award. They believed in spending money on their best people, and they budgeted $15,000 per winner for this annual incentive. The prize was a trip that the winners would attend with their spouses, as a group.

As luxurious as these trips were, the winners perceived them as more obligation than reward. Although exotic and deluxe, these were still excursions with colleagues in a business context. Everyone was on his or her office-best behavior and no one felt free to relax.

The organization decided to make a change. At the start of the year, the company distributed cards to each person in the sales organization and invited them to write down what they would do with a $15,000 prize if they won it and could spend the money any way they wanted. One salesperson dreamed of buying a Harley-Davidson motorcycle. Another wanted to spend the money on college tuition. One man wanted to fly his mother from Poland for a visit; he hadn't seen her in 15 years. The cards were gathered up and saved. At the end of the year, the winning salespeople were giving their prize money to spend on the wishes described on their cards. The cost of the award had not changed at all, but giving people the power to personalize their reward galvanized employee motivation.

The sales force sold more, sales results improved—and so did the company's cultural currency. The value of the prize to the recipients was suddenly orders of magnitude beyond the tempered satisfaction they'd felt previously. The winning salespeople were now using their prize to achieve personal and unique dreams. Within the organization, moving and inspiring stories about dreams coming true have been created and woven into the fabric of the corporate culture. This company made a Platinum Rule shift to recognize people, based on how they wanted to be motivated. By extending a transcendent level of empathy to their salespeople, the company realized immeasurable value. The impact encompassed a highly motivated workforce, a richly improved culture, and an enhanced corporate reputation.

THE REWARDS OF EMPATHY.

Relevance asks us to put our authentic talents to work in the meaningful service of our personal and professional circles. To serve with empathy means to apply our mastery in a way that is advantageous for us and for others. At its best, empathetic service does more than address a need; it can encourage transformation. Apple provided us with technology that was beautiful and user friendly; their products have transformed the way we experience communication. Phil's client, by inviting its sales force to create their own incentive motivation, transformed its employees and its culture, empowering employees with an opportunity to realize their dreams.

The only motivation with positive long-term effectiveness is self-motivation. We can't be someone's reason to change. Instead, our job is to allow empathy to guide us in asking questions that prompt thoughtful reflection—and that help people to find their own motivation for change.

This realization has had a powerful effect on us. Following our motto to become more deeply confused about more important things, we found ourselves spending less time in the answer business and more time in the question business. We have shifted from trying to bring people answers to focusing more on helping people to frame insightful questions. We don't feel worthy of providing answers, and besides, it's taxing to always be the answer guy. When "being the answer guy" is our value proposition, we create expectations that are difficult to maintain and, frankly, offer less-than-maximum benefit in the long run.

The grander gift is helping people to better frame their own issues by using the tools of empathy. Our transition from answer-centric thinking to question-centric thinking is not the result of a grand epiphany, but more a matter of emotional pragmatism. It gradually became clear that it was more practical to help people with questions.

EMPATHY AND THE NAVIGATIONAL VALUE OF CLARITY.

As we balance the demands of empathy with our needs for our own well-being, we appreciate the guidance offered by a sponsor working with the 12-step methodology. "In the treatment of addiction, your objective is to support people as they identify their own higher power," he explains. "They may believe in God, or they may believe in themselves—that's up to them. Just make sure that you don't become their surrogate higher power. You can never fulfill that responsibility. And if you don't realize that you've assumed it for someone else, it's an absolute ironclad guarantee for deep disappointment. You can't convince someone else to be better. They have to choose that themselves. I have to allow the people I counsel to move to the place where they feel the pain of not making a choice for themselves. As difficult as it is, unless they take responsibility for themselves, they are never going to get out."

We can extend empathy to those around us, but we can't be the reason for someone else to change. We can't substitute our will to want to make them better for their will to get better. They have to find their own reason.

A TACITURN FATHER'S LIFE SPEAKS VOLUMES ABOUT EMPATHY.

Phil remembers how his understanding of empathy was brought home to him in a deeply personal way when he lost his father, the unassuming man of few words.

At the funeral, Phil shared reflections about his father's life. Afterward, Phil and his wife, Julie, headed down to the church basement with friends and family to share memories over the traditional potluck of home-baked casseroles. During the gathering, five elderly gentlemen made it a point to seek out Phil and explain, with tears in their eyes, that his father was the best friend they'd known in their lives. It was an emotionally moving day.

As Phil and Julie headed home, Phil remarked that he'd had no idea that his taciturn father had so many best friends. Mulling over this revelation, he recalled a conversation about friendship that he'd had with his father several years earlier. Phil's father had explained his philosophy of friendship in four words. "Be interested, not interesting."

For Phil, those four words, and experiencing their meaning in the faces of his father's grieving friends, changed everything. He realized that a person could be drowning in intelligence and yet dying for empathy. Information can tell us what we have, and mastery can put that information into effective service, but neither information nor mastery can teach us to care. It is empathy that gives us the insight to understand how our gifts are relevant to the friends and clients we wish to serve. Phil's father valued friendship, and understood that being a good friend was about setting aside his own preoccupations and focusing his attention on the concerns that mattered to his friends.

As we loosen our self-imposed expectation that we ought to have the answers, a gratifying thing happens. When we let go of the need to "be right," we can settle into listening and asking the questions that help others unearth their needs. Encouraging others to explore their options for themselves loosens their sense of dependence on us and enables us to fully embrace the reward of being self-donational. It also happens to be the technique most likely to produce lasting positive change. Working together, asking better questions, and encouraging exploration of possible answers—these are the skills of empathy. They enable us to unearth deeper insights and support profound self-generated motivation.

From Disraeli to Phil's father, empathy's lesson is the understanding that life isn't about us. Relevance requires us to not only discover our gifts, but also, and more importantly, to learn how to give them away in a meaningful and beneficial context. Perhaps nothing exemplifies the power of empathy more than the Rule of 8,000. It's very simple. If we effect positive change for 20 people in our life, and they each have an impact on 20 more, and those people each benefit 20, suddenly, what began with us has touched the lives of 8,000 people. We don't have to solve world hunger in order to be of service. It is enough to discover the power of our own touchstone, and ground our actions in what is right and true. There's no predicting how far the effects of empathy may travel.

EMPATHY SUMMARY INSIGHTS

Empathy is the docking station of relevance. In our personal and business lives, empathy allows us to connect what we do with those who need it.

We use the definition of empathy expressed in *To Kill a Mockingbird*: **To understand a person, we have to consider things from his point of view.**

The rise of narcissism. Empathy is in decline, while narcissism is on the rise.

Compounding the rise of narcissism is the creep of commoditization. Not only are products and services being devalued, so are segments of the workforce.

Empathy as service. When we show up as authentic, empathetic human beings, we create a sense of connection with others that is impervious to commoditization.

Three levels of empathy:

- **Reactive empathy.** *This is ground-floor empathy. Someone asks for something, and we give it to him or her.*
- **Solution-based empathy.** *This is empathy that looks beyond satisfying a direct request, to create a more imaginative win–win solution.*
- **Transcendent empathy.** *This level of empathy creates a solution for a problem that hasn't even been articulated. It addresses unidentified needs and requires us to think on a much higher level about people's wants and preferences.*

Three metacomponents that develop empathy:

- **Be a student of humankind.** *Empathy begins with understanding, and understanding begins with curiosity. When we are open to others' perspectives, we are in a better position to learn about human nature.*
- **Desire to be of service.** *Once we recognize our own humanity, we can explore our communities as students of humankind and cultivate a passion to learn about what motivates others.*
- **Know how to listen.** *Good listeners step back from their own concerns, actively listening for what is important to their companions.*

The tools of empathy:
- **Humor.** *Shared laughter transforms the ordinary into a sense of appreciative intimacy.*
- **Curiosity.** *Intellectual appetite prompts us to initiate conversation with anyone, eager to experience the human spirit through a new perspective.*

The three currencies of relationships:
- **Insights:** *Insights tell us how someone else might solve an issue.*
- **Hindsights:** *Hindsights encourage us to apply life's lessons to the problem at hand.*
- **Foresights:** *Foresights inform us about how we might handle the challenges on the horizon.*

Tolerance. When our own inner resources are satisfied, we have the reserves of tolerance we need to extend our resources in empathy.
- **Dependable rituals.** *Creating repeatable patterns establishes trust and creates a sense of reliability.*
- **Transcend the need to be right.** *We tend to overestimate our abilities, but a self-serving bias won't help us work in a meaningful way for others.*
- **The discipline to pause.** *Key to the practice of empathy is the ability to rein in the urge to leap to a solution. We pause to be sure we understand the question before we start formulating answers.*
- **The rule of Five Whys.** *This question-asking technique clarifies both the nature of a problem and its solution. The concept is as simple as it sounds. We ask the question "Why?" five times.*

We have all the tools we need: we now know who we are and what we have to give. And we can identify those we are able to serve. Through action, those tools go to work allowing us to build lives that matter more.

ACTION

$$(A_u + M^2 + E) \times (\mathbf{A_c}) = R$$

Action is the engine of relevance. Without action, authenticity, mastery, and empathy are tools sitting idly in a toolbox. Our ability to gain mastery, develop empathy, and achieve authenticity can be limited by ability and fate, but we do have control over action. The first rule of paddling a canoe downriver is that in order to steer our canoe, we must be going faster than the river. And the only way to go faster than the river is to paddle hard. In the same way, if we are merely going with the flow, we will never be able to choose where we go in this world. Ultimately, there is no relevance without action.

A FEW WORDS FROM A MAN OF FEW WORDS.

As a copywriter, Tom has a particular appreciation for the witty and succinct one-liner. The snappy riposte is so much easier to appreciate than it is to generate. One of his favorites is a quote from the president who is best known for not talking at all. According to historical legend, when a woman bet Calvin Coolidge at a dinner party that she could get three words out of him, he replied, "You lose."

As taciturn as Coolidge was, there were a few topics that could move him to more than two words. He had, for example, an entire paragraph's worth of words to say about the two-word phrase "press on."

"Nothing in this world can take the place of persistence," he said. "Talent will not; nothing is more common than unsuccessful people with talent. Genius will not; unrewarded genius is almost a proverb. Education will not; the world is full of educated derelicts. Persistence and determination alone are omnipotent. The slogan 'press on' has solved and always will solve the problems of the human race."

As we've reflected on the qualities required to be relevant, these words from the man of few words insistently confront us. They remind us that no matter how authentic we are, no matter how much mastery we achieve or how much empathy we cultivate, relevance is impossible to attain without action. While our ability to gain mastery, develop empathy, and achieve authenticity can be limited by fate, we do have control over action—it is the great differentiator.

ABRAHAM LINCOLN AND THE SHINING STAR.

When Abraham Lincoln was sworn into presidential office under the stormy skies of civil war, General George B. McClellan was considered a master of military logistics in the battlefield arena—that iconic proving ground for men of action. McClellan was born to be a soldier. At the age of 13, he began studying law, but within two years came to the firm belief that he was destined for military greatness. With his father's assistance, the 15-year-old McClellan was accepted at the United States Military Academy at West Point. He distinguished himself during his studies in the theoretical principles of military tactics, and through experiences commanding surveying expeditions in the West and on assignment abroad as a military observer. By age 34, he had become the president of the Ohio and Mississippi Railroad. But civilian employment frustrated him. As the Union mobilized, McClellan was actively pursued for a state militia military command and commissioned as a major general in federal service. He was outranked only by Brevet Lieutenant General Winfield Scott, the general-in-chief.

Throughout his career, McClellan exhibited personal authenticity. He had a deep sense of who he was and the commitment to pursue the path he thought correct. His mastery was evident. He graduated second in his class at West Point. He established a reputation for military acumen during service in the Mexican-American War and was dispatched to Europe as an official observer of the siege of Sevastopol during the Crimean War. Upon his return, he wrote a manual on Russian cavalry tactics that was adopted by the United States Army. McClellan's empathy for his men was arguably his greatest strength. With the possible exception of Washington, no general in American history was held in higher esteem by those he commanded. McClellan cared deeply for his soldiers. He understood their need for leadership and discipline, and seemed to have an almost telepathic ability to give them what they needed when they needed it.

With historic events propelling the United States toward civil war, McClellan, in confident possession of authenticity, mastery, and empathy, was poised on the brink of greatness. Carl Sandburg would laud him as "the man of the hour, pointed to by events, and chosen by an overwhelming weight of public and private opinion."

The ability to act is the fourth component of relevance, and it is absolutely essential. As the engine of relevance, action operationalizes our signature strengths toward our purpose. We are what we do, not what we say we will do. As Confederate and Union armies readied for battle, the country watched to see what McClellan would do.

MIRACLES ARE HARD WORK.

Knowing what to do is not enough; we actually have to do it. Without action to send us in pursuit of our calling, our potential will languish. There are people who have high authenticity, but low competence—they don't put their gifts into action. They are called nice people, but we can't depend on them to produce results. Conversely, there are people who are highly competent—they zealously get the job done, but their methods sometimes leave a trail of broken glass. We call them empty suits. Neither path will create a relevant life. Relevance requires the development of the building blocks of authenticity, mastery, and empathy united in purposeful action. Our dreams remain dreams until we realize them through tangible intentional acts. It takes action to build a relevant life.

Minnesotan Herb Brooks had a natural aptitude for action. Chance does not seem to have figured into the trajectory of his career. Self-driven from an early age, he experienced his Great Humbling when he was the last player cut from the 1960 Olympic hockey team. Three weeks later, he sat in his living room and watched his team take the gold medal without him. Afterward, with admirable grace, he congratulated the coach who'd cut him. "Well, you must have made the right decision," Brooks said. "You won." Brooks continued to skate, setting a record by playing on eight U.S. National and Olympic teams over the next decade. He retired from playing and was later hired to coach the 1980 Olympic hockey team. Brooks seized the opportunity. Famous for observing, "Hard work beats talent when talent doesn't work hard," Brooks developed a hybrid style emphasizing creativity, teamwork, and endurance. Using "Brooksisms" like "this team isn't talented enough to win on talent alone," he shaped a group of fierce rivals from competing colleges into an uncommon team focused on representing their country—together. His team defeated the seemingly invincible Soviets in a victory dubbed the "Miracle on Ice."

The impulse to act doesn't come as naturally to all of us as it did to Minnesota's legendary hockey coach. The ancient Greeks believed that mastery, or excellence, does not prompt action. Aristotle explained that it was the other way around: good habits, cultivated through repeated action, create excellence. This is the idea that Brooks built into his philosophy: hard work would beat talent. We have seen this principle at work in mastery. We are not born with fully developed expertise; rather, we diligently practice our skills until we develop expertise. Our practice develops our mastery. In the same way, we can choose to make a habit of action. Our habit of hard work cultivates an appreciation for action that spurs us to deliver our skill to the world. Action is the difference between living a life of mattering and a life of loitering.

FORCED ACTION.

The importance of cultivating action is underscored by neurological medicine. Clinical research tells us that the brain is notoriously lazy; we literally have to force it to act. The award-winning research of behavioral neuroscientist Edward Taub demonstrated that when a stroke patient has one paralyzed arm, the brain will take the easy way out. It will rely on the function of the healthy arm instead of working to rehabilitate the injured arm. Only when the patient's healthy arm is restrained, leaving the brain no choice, will it work to regain function in the paralyzed limb. Taub discovered that our brains are disinclined to act, even when action is in our own best interest. However, as Taub's breakthrough research with stroke victims showed, we can create certain conditions that spur the brain to act.

We can create conditions to spur ourselves to act too. Studying the rule of law won't make a great litigator. It is the act of trying cases in real courtrooms with real plaintiffs and defendants and judges and juries, week after week and year after year that develops lawyers into top trial attorneys. Action follows the lessons of mastery. We have to put ourselves into situations where we must practice, where action is not an option. The surgical resident interested in learning trauma will bypass a residency at a quiet community hospital for a residency at a fast-paced Level I trauma center treating a high volume of trauma patients. A Level I trauma center residency is far more rigorous—and not particularly glamorous—but the intensive culture of a dedicated trauma center will cultivate the decisive judgment and action required of a surgeon specializing in trauma. By choice or by chance, we must actively test our limits to know our capabilities.

GENERAL IN ACTION VS. GENERAL INACTION.

We aren't wise enough to guess about the balance between choice and chance in developing the habits of action, but we suspect that both dynamics play a role. Sometimes, like Brooks, we choose to take action, and sometimes, like Brooks' Olympic hockey team, action is thrust upon us. The interplay between choice and chance is present early in the careers of McClellan and Ulysses S. Grant. While McClellan studied theoretical strategy at West Point, Grant was earning a reputation as a fearless horseman.

Both McClellan and Grant had their first experience of active battle in the Mexican-American War. McClellan arrived at the Rio Grande bristling with weapons, but too late to take part in the American victory at Monterrey. Then he was laid low for a month with dysentery and malaria. Meanwhile, Grant, serving as quartermaster, had surged to the front lines in four battles before McClellan was even dispatched to the Rio Grande. By the time Grant fought at Monterrey, he was a seasoned cavalryman with a reputation for braving snipers' bullets while galloping, as he later wrote, "on the side of my horse furthest from the enemy, and with only one foot holding to the cantle of the saddle." While McClellan lay ill in his tent, Grant was promoted twice for bravery. As he advanced, Grant studied the command styles of his superiors. McClellan mastered the theories of warfare, and observed them in action abroad, but he had seldom been pressed to apply his knowledge in active battle. Grant, on the other hand, emerged from the Mexican-American War with an understanding of battle forged through combat—and a cultivated habit for actively engaging the enemy.

McClellan's actions were frequently motivated by a remarkable sense of self-importance. From the earliest days of his career, he demonstrated a tendency for insubordination that came to characterize his relationship with Lincoln. As the commander of Union forces, McClellan outraged his superior, General-in-Chief Winfield Scott, by refusing to divulge details about his strategic planning, or even standard information about troop strengths and dispositions. When Scott finally resigned in frustration, McClellan took on the role of general-in-chief on top of his role as army commander. To Lincoln's concern about the "vast labor" of the dual role, McClellan responded, "I can do it all." McClellan overestimated his strengths and ignored his limitations.

AN OBJECT AT REST ...

Time after time, when McClellan had General Robert E. Lee outnumbered and outmaneuvered, he refused to take the fight to him. Lincoln wryly noted that McClellan was "always almost ready to fight." McClellan commanded not only the largest army ever gathered on the North American continent, but also the best trained, the best equipped, and the best organized. Yet, his battlefield style was bewilderingly overcautious. For months, Confederate General Joseph Johnston kept McClellan's forces at bay with logs that had been painted black to look like cannons. McClellan consistently overestimated the strength of the troops arrayed against him, and repeatedly refused to reinforce attacks with reserve troops, prompting Lincoln to remark, "If General McClellan isn't going to use his army, I'd like to borrow it for a time." McClellan had talent, genius, and education in abundance, but hampered by his hubris and his crippling hesitancy to act, his strengths were completely impotent.

AN OBJECT IN MOTION ...

Grant lacked virtually all of McClellan's laudable qualities. He graduated near the bottom of his class at West Point. He was slovenly, pathetic at business, and then there was the drinking. But even as he accepted a position to recruit and train volunteer units for the Union army, his superiors were describing him as "a man of dogged persistence and iron will." Grant was a man of action.

Grant may not have had McClellan's stellar pedigree when it came to the qualities of authenticity, empathy, and mastery, but he had enough of those qualities to be extremely relevant when he put them into action. Grant had cultivated the habits of action from his earliest days in combat. And while both men were authentic in their own ways, Grant lacked McClellan's hubris. When it came to empathy, both men possessed it, but the focus of each man's empathic ability was radically different. McClellan had an exceptional capacity to stand in the shoes of his troops; Grant was considered almost callous to the destruction of life under his command. But Grant possessed an empathetic canniness even more critical to a military leader—he was able to stand in the shoes of his adversary. Grant's ability to anticipate Lee was a key element to his success on the battlefield. Also, Grant's military mastery was not chained to convention; he had studied his commanders during the heat of battle and learned from them. The habits of action under pressure prepared him to push beyond his comfort zone and adapt to the evolution of the art of war. While McClellan applied the nuance of the Napoleonic tactics he had observed in Europe, Grant shifted to the new calculus of wars of attrition. For Grant, the war was a chess game. He understood that every time Lee lost a piece, that piece was gone forever. Every time Grant lost a piece, he knew he had another soldier in reserve to put on the board.

Authenticity, mastery, and empathy become relevant only when they are conscripted into action's cause. Without action, the qualities of authenticity, mastery, and empathy are moot. Any action is better than no action at all.

Grant demonstrated that an average pedigree fueled by active persistence will outperform a brilliant but frozen pedigree every time. Action can even overcome gaps in qualifications. When confronted with rumors that Grant was a drunkard, Lincoln replied, "If it (alcohol) makes fighting men like Grant, then find out what he drinks and send my other commanders a case!"

Ultimately, the difference between these generals came down to action. Grant took it. McClellan dithered. Action is still the difference between a relevant life and a life lived on the misty sidelines. Act, or live a life that is never able to matter.

THE RACE GOES TO THE SWIFT.

Action demands that we cultivate the habits of tenacity and perseverance. It does not indulge those who insist on waiting for their muse, or for "the proper mood" to descend. In fact, when we live a life waiting for the right moment, we run the risk of loitering in the starting blocks until the race has passed us by. Loitering becomes a habit of inaction, and breeds doubt and fear. Runners begin in the blocks and wait for the gun to go off. In the race of life, we can't wait for someone else to shoot the gun. Life rewards action. We can't think our way to a new way of living. We have to live our way to a new way of thinking. The Civil War was one of the first truly industrial wars, employing mass-produced weapons and a deadly new way of fighting. McClellan tried to think his way through each engagement, refusing to act until he felt absolutely certain of his readiness—which he almost never did. Grant, on the other hand, advanced relentlessly, demonstrating what Lincoln called "the dogged pertinacity ... that wins" even in the face of staggering carnage.

McClellan may have felt secure in his tent, loath to move against the enemy troops whose numbers he had overestimated, but the security he felt was more hubris than wise judgment. As history has demonstrated, he did not have unlimited time to wait for his right moment. None of us do. When McClellan hesitated for too long, he was swept aside by those willing to seize the imperfect present moment.

Our dreams of greatness—or maybe just of doing our best—will be only dreams until we create momentum in our lives by taking action. We may know that we must forgo those extra helpings if we want to lose a pound, but until we put down our fork and say "no thanks" to another serving, the weight will not come off. We may know that a trip to visit our aging parents will enable us to connect with them and express our gratitude, but unless we get in the car and start driving in their direction, they will not experience the appreciation we want them to feel. Our lives are filled with examples of what is called the "knowing-doing gap." The gap represents opportunities squandered. Action bridges the gap.

CHOOSE YOUR ROLE: GREEK DRAMA.

Our actions are a reflection of the decisions we make about who we want to be and how we want to live. Our habits of action dedicate us to a way of being; they become the driver that keeps us on the path we have chosen for ourselves. Few of us may distinguish ourselves through spectacular deeds, but we can be heroic in the quiet acts of everyday life. We can extend a helping hand, offer a kind word, and meet our difficulties bravely. Action needn't be heroic; it simply has to move us along our authentic path.

The ancient Greeks discovered that the formula to put on a great play was a reflection of the roles we human beings choose to enact in our professional and personal lives. They refined our choices to just a few basic roles with clearly defined purposes. Some of us assume smaller and humbler roles by choice. Others of us may play small parts, but dream of seeing our name in lights someday. As we ponder the habits we are going to choose in life, the roles defined in Greek theater provide an informative—and entertaining—guide.

The Audience. We pay for our ticket. Applaud at appropriate times. Some of us watch others living out their dreams, and we fill the air with opinions about how we could have done better.

Relevance: more than zero, but only if there are lots of empty seats.

Member of the Chorus. Our main job is to fill in the narrative necessary to move the story along, express the characters' hidden fears or motives, and provide a warning to the protagonist as needed. Typically, faceless and nameless members of the chorus have no individual voice to claim; they are the very definition of a commodity. Chorus members are the functionaries of the modern world. The world doesn't work without us, but, with perhaps a very few exceptions, the world does not notice us either.

Relevance: needed, but individually we are incredibly replaceable. Almost anyone can join the chorus if willing to accept the very lowest of wages.

Tritagonist. We are up on stage mingling with the stars, but we aren't quite one of them. The job of tritagonists is to add some color, fill in as needed, and, at critical moments, play an important part in the action. Tritagonists are pressured by competition from above and below. Whether or not we can reach the summit is determined in part by fate and in part by our own ability to become significantly relevant.

Relevance: at key times, absolutely relevant, but most often irrelevant. In order for tritagonists to become truly relevant, we must seek to fulfill our potential.

Deuteragonist. This player is second banana, the sidekick. Deuteragonists complement the protagonist and are critical to the success or failure of the hero in the leading role. We are trustworthy and dependable, but at the end of the day, the story is really not about us. We have a genuine shot at being the center of the story if we take the steps to enhance our relevance.

Relevance: significantly relevant to the success of any venture.

Antagonist. Enter the troublemaker, the player who creates obstacles for the protagonist. The antagonist can create trouble with everything from malice to stupidity. We poison the culture, hamper success, and are capable of dragging everyone into muck, mire, and malaise. Sometimes, we see the antagonist when we look in the mirror. Regrettably, we are often the antagonists in our own lives. It is so much easier to relegate blame to other people who "have a problem." The reality is that we all "have a problem" and that problem is us.

Relevance: less than zero. Elimination or reclamation are the only options.

Protagonist. Here, at last, is our main character: the star. This is the person with whom we most identify. The protagonist is the one who makes things happen in the story. If we are heroes, we overcome obstacles and achieve our goal. If not, the story becomes a tragedy.

The problem with being a protagonist is that we are the one who succeeds or fails. Everything is on the line; it goes with the territory. Fear of being the one who takes the risk and fails is often the one reason that so many choose to play a lesser role in life. Being a protagonist means taking risks. Sometimes risk is rewarded with success, and sometimes risk results in failure. But as mastery has taught us, failure is necessary to growth. The protagonists in life make things happen despite the obstacles.

Relevance: utmost. Sought after because they dedicate themselves to accomplishing their goals, these are the people who step up to make contributions within their sphere of influence.

BE THE PROTAGONIST IN YOUR OWN STORY.

There's one directive Tom frequently shares: "Be the protagonist in your own story." We have to overcome the obstacles that invariably hamper the path to success. It means rejecting the notion that we are victims of the Fates and those around us. We are the ones who determine how the story will end and who will take responsibility for the outcome. Being the protagonist in our own story doesn't mean that we have to be the leader of our company or our community. Not everyone is born with Grant's keen aptitude for action or Lincoln's gift for leadership. But we can choose to step into the leading role on the one path we really do control—our own.

Phil has a great phrase that encapsulates the natural benefit of being a protagonist and achieving relevance. He says, "In your life, you can either be a free agent or a journeyman." The free agent sets his or her terms, because the service offered by a free agent is crafted to deliver unique authenticity. The journeyman is forced to accept what is offered, because his or her services reflect the status quo. In order to matter more, we have to define our gifts in a way that distinguishes them as valuable and unique.

ACTION'S ROLE IN THE FORMULA OF RELEVANCE.

Recall our formula for relevance: the sum of authenticity and mastery and empathy, times action $((Au+M^2+E) \times (Ac) = R)$. Notice that the first three qualities are added together and then multiplied by action. When we total our authentic gifts, areas of mastery, and empathetic skills, the sum is the mass of our potential. But mass won't move itself. To move, we need the velocity of action. All four dynamics are necessary, but it is action that carries us from potential to significance in the world. Mass times velocity equals action. The decision to put the mass of relevance into action is the great differentiator between those who dream and those who do.

When we possess both the mass of potential and the velocity of action, our equation can work in all sorts of ways. For example, a high level of velocity can make up for a lack of mass. Grant's academic work at West Point showed less-than-desirable mastery, and his drinking may have marred his authenticity, but his military leadership was marked by sheer driving force. His capacity for action led to victory after victory, and more than compensated for his shortcomings in mass. In the same way, a glittering mass of talent and skill can compensate for less vigorous velocity. It took Theodor S. Geisel nine months to write the 1,629-word story we know and love as *The Cat in the Hat*. That works out to about six words per day. No one would contest the fact that the result of Geisel's imaginative genius, translated into 12 languages and selling more than 11 million copies, was worth every minute of the time he required to craft his beloved tale. Powerful velocity can make up for less mass, and an abundance of mass can make up for measured velocity, but we need enough mass and at least some measure of velocity. Try putting imaginary numbers in for authenticity, mastery, and empathy. No matter how high a number we come up with, if we multiply it by zero action, our ultimate relevance is zero. Zero times even a billion is still zero. Ultimately, there is no relevance without action. It's frightening how much action determines our relevance.

DIRECTION MATTERS.

When we have identified and developed our passions, and have made the choice to actively use them, there's still one more detail to attend to. Action can propel us in any number of directions. Action doesn't always steer us in the direction of relevance—some actions can be self-sabotaging. We may intend to go in one direction, yet choose actions that push us away from our goals instead of toward them. We can be the antagonists, as well as the protagonists, of our own lives. This is the lesson that McClellan learned too late.

The building block of authenticity is important precisely because it gives us the tools to avoid the role of the self-limited antagonist. As we reflect on the actions we might take at any point in life, we reap the benefits of having gone through authenticity's process of unflinchingly assessing our limitations as well as our assets. When we honestly evaluate both weaknesses and strengths, we create the opportunity to cultivate habits founded on self-awareness. These are the habits that prevent our weaknesses from becoming liabilities.

We cultivate and exercise authenticity so that when it is time to choose our path of action, we'll have at least some judgment, gleaned from experience, to guide us. With hindsight's clear vision, we can identify McClellan's stumble in authenticity. Every time his pride brought him into conflict with his superiors, he had the opportunity to assess his actions and reflect on whether his pride was serving him. But McClellan did not come to grips with his hubris. Someone else was always to blame for his shortcomings. The difference between the two generals is illustrated in a letter that Grant sent to Lincoln. He wrote, "Should my success be less than I desire, and expect, the least I can say is, the fault is not with you." Over time, McClellan's regrettable habit of playing the part of subversive antagonist became a fatal flaw. Combined with his inability to act when action was required, McClellan's hubris and inertia sabotaged his own ambitions. Despite all of the accomplishments he had accumulated, in the absence of action, relevance remained beyond his reach.

THE DECISION TO OPERATIONALIZE
OUR SIGNATURE STRENGTHS.

Just as authenticity has its challenges, so too does action. We are inundated with options, and this may tempt us to postpone a choice. Do we use a gift for critical thinking to lead a company, or to litigate in a courtroom? Will we take our surgical skills to a part of the world where they are desperately needed, or refine our subspecialty expertise in a focused practice that handles complex cases beyond the skill of the general surgeon? Committing to a single path means closing the door to other options. This is difficult, because a part of us yearns for the illusion that no opportunity is lost. And yet, if we do not make a choice, circumstances will choose for us.

Decisions are not the result of happenstance, inattention, or neglect. They are conscious choices between legitimate and rational alternatives, born of deliberation. We cannot preserve all of our options indefinitely. When we postpone decisions, we are relinquishing control of our lives and putting the reins of our future in the hands of chance. Better to make the choices that close some doors but help us realize the dreams we have conceived than to languish in possibilities that slowly fade to nothing for lack of pursuit. Our dreams won't reach fruition simply because they are possible at a certain point in time. Time marches on. If we don't choose our dreams, time will choose them for us.

We have identified a set of tools to help keep us clearly connected to our core values, cultivating the habits that move us forward, and defining the direction that keeps us on course. We use them to help with the decision-making process and to keep our actions aligned with our core values. Our suggestions are not comprehensive; we don't intend them to be. Embarking on the journey of relevance is not just about having answers; it's also about exploring the fascinating questions that come up along the way. There is one visionary, especially, who excelled at spinning fascinating questions into extraordinary relevance. He helped transform the digital age and mesmerized us all with his elegant and beautifully designed devices.

PASSION DIRECTING ACTION.

Steve Jobs was born in the counterculture milieu of San Francisco and raised in Silicon Valley in the 1960s and 1970s, just as the fledgling potential of the computer emerged. He used a computer for the first time when he was about 10. It was only a teletype printer with a keyboard attached to it, but the young Jobs was captivated. He was convinced that computer technology would change the world, and determined to build a computer of his own. When we watch the interview where Jobs recalls phoning Bill Hewlett as a precocious 12-year-old looking for spare computer parts, it is obvious that Jobs discovered his authentic passion at a very young age and wasted no time putting passion into action. His literal call to action landed him a summer job at Hewlett-Packard. Jobs' affinity for acting on passion had opened a door to his future, and would later pay off in vitally important and unanticipated ways.

ACTION INTENSIFIED BY FOCUS.

The compulsive rush of modern life hardly facilitates directed action. Our world is one of constant disruption. There never seems to be enough time to complete our list of tasks. Distraction surrounds us. Our phones are ringing, our email boxes are filling up, our calendars are packed with appointments, and there are always unanticipated fires and emergencies lunging into our day to deflect our focus.

When our lives are thoroughly booked from morning until late in the evening, it's situationally impossible to stumble upon solitude and time to reflect by happy chance. Unless we deliberately carve out time to prioritize our objectives, how do we chart a course of action grounded in considered authenticity? How do we rise above the fray to review our navigation and keep ourselves directionally on track with our goals? How do we do everything we can about the few things that matter instead of scattering what we do over many things that don't matter?

Our term for the challenge posed by overscheduled lives filled with demands pulling us in multiple directions is "reflection loss." In the throes of amazing technological advances, opportunities for connection have multiplied, but so have opportunities for distraction. The consequences of non-reflection can be disastrous. Thoughtful action requires clear, deliberate decision making grounded in a solid foundation of authentic self-awareness.

Information is at our fingertips in overwhelming quantities, and organizing it into data helps a little, but not enough. If we spend enough time sifting through information and data, we may come to knowledge. But if we are committed to deeper insight about the dynamics of our lives, we need time to reflect on the consequences of our decisions, observe whether those consequences move us toward our goals, and then learn to hone our actions to be more effective in the future. Reflection turns intelligence into relevance.

ANOTHER REASON TO PAUSE (BUT NOT FOR LONG).

There's no getting around it. We need to find time to reflect. Decisions about the course of our life's journey encompass a complexity of perspectives and potential outcomes. It takes time to open intuition to options we may not be considering, but perhaps should be.

Constructing an actionable vision for our lives requires more than collecting data, information, and other people's ideas. It demands that we do our own thinking. In order to make the decisions that determine our life path, we need to concentrate, imagine our future, and develop our own ideas about how we might get there. This is not a task that can be accomplished in 10-second bursts while juggling four other assignments and fielding interruptions.

Time is our most valuable asset, and the asset most at risk. As valuable as financial resources are, we can earn more money to replace what we spend. We cannot replace a single moment of our time. Once we have spent it, it is gone forever. Each week, we have about 100 waking hours to spend in pursuit of what we define as meaningful. Each of us chooses where we invest our only-once-in-a-lifetime hours.

Set aside the time to map a path. We have a deep desire to live a satisfying life that engages our passions and matters to others. Sometimes, it takes a tragedy to focus us on contemplating our purpose. Sometimes, a mentor guides us to self-discovery.

And sometimes, like Steve Jobs, we are born at the right time and in the right place to discover a captivating interest that burns so brightly before us that we are compelled to follow. Whether we are set on our path by heartbreak, guidance, or inspiration, the journey is never mindless. There will always be actions required of us, and decisions to be made along the way.

WHAT?

When we are able to apply uninterrupted concentration to an issue, we prepare ourselves to address three questions that can move us from decision making to action:

- **What?** What decision do we want to make, and where will it take us?

- **So what?** How will the results of our decision move us closer to, or further from, our objectives?

- **Now what?** If we make a decision that moves us forward, can we refine it to make it more effective in the future? If our decision is unhelpful, what do we need to do to correct our course?

Battles need a plan of action, and so does a relevant life. We can't map out our direction until we know where we are and where we want to go. Complexity fatigue, activity addiction, and lack of time collude to distract us and prevent us from doing this valuable analysis. Unless we are regularly reviewing our experiences, their meaning, and their implications, we are in danger of losing sight of the big picture. Our big picture is our personal foundation, and effective action is grounded in the foundation-based habits that move us forward.

CULTIVATE HABITS OF REPEATED ACTION.

When we make a habit of acting on the interests arising out of our authentic passions, our enthusiasm can open doors before we even realize the potential that lies beyond them. Youthful determination to build a computer propelled Jobs down a path that introduced him to the business of technology, just as Grant's determination to fight on the front in the Mexican-American War gave him the opportunity to study firsthand the actions of commanding generals in the thick of battle.

Acting on our interests refines our understanding of what we are good at and what we value. The experiences we have along the way sometimes introduce us to new values that enhance and enlarge our vision. The lessons we learn through habits of action test our understanding and teach us to identify what matters in our life. Babbage had conceived his "Analytical Engine" as a device that would perform complex mathematical sums. Ada Lovelace understood that this invention could be far more, and demonstrated its potential through her active development of the first computer algorithm. A century later, the world thought of the personal computer as a fascinating but impractical amusement; Jobs saw in it the potential to spearhead a technical revolution. In both cases, habits of action cultivated early in life laid the foundation for unique skill sets able to carve a path beyond the mundane and into the relevant.

CULTIVATE FOCUSED DIRECTION.

Relevance requires us to do more than maintain the status quo. If we want to matter more, we have to think independently, creatively, and flexibly. The changing nature of the world requires us to deploy our authentic skills in fluid and sometimes unfamiliar situations.

As we test the limits of our talents, it is helpful to remember the notion of majoring in the majors, instead of the minors. Outstanding individuals, able to develop deep expertise in multiple disciplines, are rare. We measure the distance between polymaths in centuries. Much more frequently, invaluable contributions have come from men and women who chose to develop the one remarkable and distinguishing talent that outshone their other skills.

Raised by prominent Harvard physician and literary scholar Oliver Wendell Holmes Sr., Holmes Jr. loved literature and served with distinction in the Union army. But the younger Holmes' legal aptitude towered over his other interests. Appointed to the Supreme Court by President Theodore Roosevelt, Holmes is recognized as one of the few Supreme Court justices in history chosen strictly for his contribution to the law, and is one of the three most cited American legal scholars of the 20th century. Mark Twain's multiple careers included printer, riverboat pilot, and miner, but it was the singular wit and satire of his literary contribution that won him an enduring place in American literary history. Jonas Salk seemed destined to the research bench. He followed his early interest in science into the study of viruses, saving countless lives as the creator of the first polio vaccine.

We are going to have to make decisions about where we focus our action. Having a multitude of choices is wonderful. Having to make a decision about which of these choices we develop—that's hard. But on the road to relevance, it is highly unlikely that we will be relevant in a dozen different disciplines. If relevance is our goal, we are going to have to exercise discernment and winnow down our choices to the authentic gift we can hone to the highest level of mastery. Without this focus, we risk dividing our direction, dissipating our effectiveness, and becoming the jack-of-all-trades who is master of none.

THE WORLD BELONGS TO DOERS.

Mattering more means actively doing more. We can't simply maintain the routine. We must ask questions, not just answer them. We must set goals, but also give some thought to whether the goals we set are worth achieving. A fundamental distinction between the relevant and the irrelevant is that relevant people choose to use their time in an intentional way.

When Steve Jobs struck up a friendship with Steve Wozniak as a teenager, Wozniak was already a gifted programmer. They experimented with computer projects and pulled a few infamous practical jokes together. When they built a digital blue box—able to make free phone calls anywhere in the world—and called the pope, their prank delivered a life-altering lesson. "Blue boxing" taught them that though they were just kids in California, they had the capability to build something that could control billions of dollars of global infrastructure. This realization inspired the vision that became the Apple computer. Their vision prepared them, during a chance visit to the Xerox Palo Alto Research Center (PARC), to recognize technology imbued with transcendent empathy when they saw it.

Long before Jobs and Wozniak set up shop in the garage, a young engineer named Douglas Engelbart was dreaming dreams of changing the world. He quit his job, earned a Ph.D. at Berkeley, and went to work for the Stanford Research Institute. Envisioning a computer with the capability to create, revise, and spellcheck documents, he introduced the concept of computer windows. And then he invented tools with which to navigate these windows, tools that would feel innately comfortable and familiar to the user. Engelbart spoke of computer users as knowledge workers. The tools his team created for them to use included hypertext and the ingeniously simple-to-use point-and-click computer mouse.

But then Engelbart lost his funding. Members of his team defected to a nearby research and development lab, Xerox PARC. By the time Engelbart's department was sold to Tymshare, he was the only remaining member of his team. Although he continued to invent, without the support to bring his remarkable products to market, he slipped into obscurity. Engelbart's vision was transcendently empathetic, but it was held hostage by a company unwilling to take action and bring it to market.

Jobs and Wozniak, however, instantly recognized Engelbart's innovations as the brilliant game-changers they were. The two visionary pranksters sprang into action, and that made all the difference.

We can't act until we know who we are and what we believe. Our sense of purpose may be cultivated through a habit of long walks or weekend retreats. It may come through attentive work that sparks inspiration, or time spent reading and engrossed in new ideas. Another pathway to clarity can come through intimate conversation with a trusted friend whose presence invites us to explore ideas in confidence. Any of these courses of action—and the list is not inclusive—can become a practiced habit that sets the stage for directed action.

If we want to honor relevance and activate directional action, we use our hours to vote deeply and with intention. We support the goals we value and guard against the distractions of endless emails and Internet trivia. We are living in a time when it has never been easier to slip into trivial distractions, but the good news is that we have a choice. It is within our power to commit to spending our hours wisely.

ACTION TURNS INSANELY GREAT IDEAS INTO INSANELY GREAT PRODUCTS.

At the age of 25, Jobs and Wozniak were laser-focused on a single goal: creating a personal computer that anyone could use, and everyone would want. "The way that we're going to ratchet up our species," explained Jobs, "is to take the best and spread it around to everybody so everybody grows up with better things and starts to understand the subtlety of these better things." The co-founders of Apple believed in exposing themselves to the finest things that humans have done, and incorporating those riches into Apple's products. Jobs loved Picasso's observation, "Good artists copy. Great artists steal." In 1979, Apple came across a treasure trove of ideas that were begging to be stolen.

Engelbart's former colleagues had joined what was reputed to be the best team of computer scientists in the country. Xerox PARC was creating computer technology of astonishing inventiveness. Ivan Sutherland of MIT envisioned and developed a drawing program called Sketchpad, operated with a lightpen. The accessible appeal of this tool inspired another gifted PARC programmer, Alan Kay, to tinker with a personal computer. The interface in his first attempt was dreadful, but shining through the shortcomings were the tiny pictures Kay had developed to guide users—he had created the computer icon. Reconceiving the computer screen as a desk, and each of Engelbart's windows as pieces of paper on the desk, Kay hit upon the idea of overlapping and stacking the windows, just as papers were stacked on a desk. His "desktop" metaphor describes computers to this day. The PARC scientists refined the insight of the seamless intuitive desktop in myriad ways. The tools they developed functioned with convivial ease and offered heretofore unimagined capacity to store knowledge in written, artistic, musical, and animated form.

Stepping into the shoes of the personal computer user, PARC built on Kay's icon concept to extend the desktop metaphor. Their visual "tools"—a printer, a trash can, a file folder—expanded the function of the computer desktop. In addition to the graphical user interface, this team was responsible for laser printers, Ethernet, object-oriented programming, and the refinement of the mouse. The product developers were incredibly masterful. In a deft leap of empathy, they designed a computer screen that reflected the user's real life. With exceptional intuition, they developed the tools destined to become the digital world's navigational landscape.

But we don't buy computers or software from the Xerox Palo Alto Research Center. The PARC researchers created with visionary mastery and transcendent user empathy, but they never acted on what they'd done. These scientists saw themselves as pure researchers. They knew they were pioneers on the forefront of computer technology, but they were publishing their discoveries in journals. They couldn't envision the heady and expensive prototypes they had created as belonging in every office and home in the country. The PARC scientists lived in a land of interesting ideas. They didn't have the impetus to bring their work to the market.

For Jobs and Wozniak, bringing computer innovation to market was the primary focus. Ideas mattered, first and foremost, as features to enhance the salability of Apple computers. They were building a personal computer industry. They developed a slew of brilliant ideas. What they didn't develop, they borrowed.

Rumors about the work being done at PARC had reached Steve Jobs. He negotiated a deal with PARC's parent company that included a demo of some of the research center's inventions. When he reminisced about that visit, Jobs described being so overcome by PARC's graphical user interface that he couldn't take in anything else. He intuitively knew that he was looking at the future of the personal computer. PARC's treasures had been revealed to a team who knew how to act on its inventions.

On the 15-minute drive back to Apple, the Apple team was already speculating about how long it would take to incorporate PARC's ideas into their own computer. Jobs gathered his best people and began the process of re-creating the innovations he'd seen. The product designers at PARC understood people and they created incredibly accessible products—but their inaction gave Apple an opening. The Apple programmers took PARC's ideas, re-created them, and improved them. Just as Grant charged past McClellan to win the Civil War, Apple adapted PARC's concepts to contribute to sea changes in the music, film, and personal computer industries.

The story of Apple's adaptation of the PARC ideas captures the essence of relevance. A transcendent idea matters, but is only one step along the road to mattering more. Like authenticity, the idea reveals the potential—but potential is not sufficient. Between the idea and its final realization exists a tremendous amount of dedicated work. Like an authentic skill that is honed to mastery, Apple's ideas changed and grew as they were developed. Products never emerged in exactly the form in which they were originally imagined. Trade-offs had to be made. Apple's computer team majored in the majors, producing products that rose above the commoditized fray.

PUT YOUR TOOLS TO WORK.

The tools of relevance put us on the path, but there's no predictable outcome or guarantee of success. Like Apple's personal computer design, any master skill in practice is about comprehending myriad elements and fitting them together in inspired ways that satisfy the objective. It was the combination of authenticity, mastery, and customer empathy that made PARC's tools so extraordinary. But it took the action-oriented Apple team to incorporate those tools into the brilliant computer that revolutionized our lives.

ACTION SUMMARY INSIGHTS

Action is the engine of relevance.

Nothing can take the place of persistence.

Authenticity, mastery, and empathy become relevant only when they are conscripted into action's cause. Without action, they are moot.

Action demands that we cultivate tenacity and perseverance.

Be the protagonist in your own story. We are not victims of fate. We determine how our story will end and we have responsibility for our story's outcome.

Direction matters. Action can propel us in any number of directions. We must choose actions that push us in the direction of our goals.

When we are able to pause and reflect on our life's direction, we prepare ourselves to address three questions that can move us from decision making to action:

- **What?** *What decision do we want to make, and where will it take us?*
- **So what?** *How will the results of our decision move us closer to, or further from, our objectives?*
- **Now what?** *If we make a decision that moves us forward, can we refine it to make it more effective in the future? If our decision is unhelpful, what do we need to do to correct our course?*

RELEVANCE SUMMATION

We have a shot at mattering more when we snap together the four essential dynamics of relevance:

Authenticity: identifying what we are good at.

Mastery: turning what we are good at into what we are great at.

Empathy: recognizing what we have to offer that is valued by others.

Action: going out and doing it.

None of these dynamics are new ground. But in combination, authenticity with mastery and empathy multiplied by action gives us relevance. It's a simple formula to state, but like many formulas, a bit more difficult to understand. In the real world, it can be a lifetime's work to execute. However, if we really want to matter more, this is the challenge before us.

We have explored the relationships between these four dynamics. With our formula in hand, we find ourselves thinking about whether we measure up. We look in the mirror, and with every pound and wrinkle we add, we wonder: "Are we still relevant? Are we still viable? Are we still even visible? Does our life's journey serve others?"

In a sense, we are all on the yellow brick road, or sizing up the shadows in Plato's cave, in search of authenticity. As the walls of triviality close in, will we surrender to the shadows of mediocrity, or will we reach out with self-understanding and empathy to matter more? In the darkest part of her journey through the forest, Dorothy exchanged support with her companions. We too have the opportunity to embrace connection with our own fellow travelers.

Phil's father understood the power of connection. He knew that the strength of our connections, with self and with others, was a reflection of our relevance. He earned, he learned, and he returned. He left life's campsite cleaner than he found it. At the end of his life, Reuben Styrlund was more concerned with his relevance than he was about his life itself.

OUR AUTHENTIC GIFTS.

Can we identify and understand our authenticity with the clarity that Teddy Roosevelt brought to scrutinizing his own gifts? Are we honest enough to use scales instead of mirrors to measure our strengths and honestly admit our limitations? Like Avis, can we frankly own our weaknesses and be forthright about the skills we wished we had—but know we don't?

When we discover the unique gifts that come naturally to us, will we polish them to excellence and take the next step on the journey to relevance?

OUR AUTHENTIC GIFTS MADE GREAT.

Ada Lovelace found her authentic programming gifts and honed them to mastery in a world where women with mathematical aptitude defied societal norms. Theodor Seuss Geisel rose to Spaulding's challenge to create a mesmerizing story for children. Understanding that mastery is not a sprint, he spent nine months crafting *The Cat in the Hat*—a classic that delights children to this day. The musicians of Tin Pan Alley embraced the discipline of limitations to compose timeless standards that move us the way only soulfully written music can. American physicist Richard Feynman's playful amusement with the notion of wobbly plates led him to insights worthy of a Nobel Prize.

OUR AUTHENTIC GIFTS MADE GREAT FOR OTHERS.

With authenticity and mastery in play, can we take the next step and feel our way into the shoes of another person so that we can look out at the world with more empathetic eyes?

Harper Lee's novel modeled empathy in the quiet decency of Atticus Finch, in its defense of victims of prejudice, and through its support for outcasts living on the fringes of society. The 3M Company reached out and invited its customers to explore the possibilities of an accidental quirky adhesive. The ubiquitous sticky note emerged precisely because 3M was open to seeing their odd discovery through their customers' eyes. Tolkien developed his deep understanding of the human condition by tracking the mysteries of our yearnings through black ink on white paper bound in hundreds of library volumes, and discussing his discoveries with an intellectually curious circle of intimate friends. Disraeli used empathy to transform his skills as a master conversationalist into an irresistible gift for making his companions feel brilliant.

OUR AUTHENTIC GIFTS MADE GREAT FOR OTHERS BY ACTION MAKES US MATTER MORE.

And with authenticity clarified, mastery practiced, and empathy embraced, will we turn the key in the engine of relevance and heed Thomas Jefferson's call to action? "Do you want to know who you are?" Jefferson demands. "Don't ask. Act! Action will delineate and define you."

McClellan was always almost ready to act, and his inability to gather his gifts and leap out of the starting blocks and onto the field proved to be the difference between his ignominy and Grant's victory. As one who made a practice of cultivating the habits of action, Grant could not understand McClellan's hesitation, remarking, "McClellan is to me one of the mysteries of the war."

The outcome of McClellan's inaction would not surprise Minnesota's revered hockey coach Herb Brooks, however. Herb knew that hard work would beat talent, and he brought home Olympic gold to prove his point. The Apple team went even further—when they saw the fruits of empathetic invention languishing in PARC, they stole the spark of creative genius, re-created it, and launched it with fanfare into a captivated world. Action gathers up the fruits of our labors and ensures that our work will not be for naught.

THE FATHER WHO MATTERED MORE.

Phil's father longed to matter, and his longing launched us on this journey. Reuben Styrlund lived the dynamics that we've described. He understood his skills, his values, and his priorities. He was authentically curious and interested in people's stories. He mastered the art of drawing people out, and treated their stories and confessions with profound empathy. These were his arts, and he put them into action as he went about his days. He always had a kind word for a stranger and time to listen to a friend. His genuine interest in others made him relevant to others, and for others.

His motto was, "Be interested, not interesting." When we are interested, people see us as interesting. And when others find us interesting, we are relevant.

We all long to matter, and we long to be remembered. When a team at the University of Indiana conducted research to understand how we remember, they found that our mind doesn't remember experiences the way that a film records experiences. We don't remember everything. Instead, we remember the highs, the lows, and the endings—with emphasis on endings. For some reason, our mind has a unique fascination with how things end.

IN THE END, MATTER MORE.

We know that Grant was not the brightest star at West Point, and that he was not immune to the temptations of the bottle, but his faults are eclipsed by his single-minded determination to lead his troops to victory, preserving the Union and subsequently winning the highest office in the land. The glory of victory softens our view of past frailties. We remember the scrappy guys who started their computer company in Steve Jobs' garage, with their meteoric rise to fame, the rocky road to Jobs' ousting from Apple, and his triumphant return. Most of all, we remember the culmination of Apple's vision; sleek laptops, iPods, and iPhones have transformed the way we interact with our world. Jobs may not have been the easiest man to work for, but the memory of the man is gilded by the genius of the technology he delivered.

When the ending is fantastic, that's how our mind remembers the journey, so it behooves us to be very intentional about how we close chapters in our lives. Whether the chapter involves a relationship, a job, or a project, we benefit when we end things with grace and consideration. When we think about the action we invest in authenticity, mastery, and empathy, the impact we make hinges on how we orchestrate conclusions along the journey. Do we want to make an impact that will be remembered? Then we must pay attention to how we end things. End well because endings matter.

Relevance is a choice we make to employ our gifts in the service of others. History shows us that we can make a choice to matter more. For some of us, the steps of our journey will mark the pages of history; for others, the journey will be a quieter but no less important matter. On this journey, significance eludes measurement; seemingly small acts can move subtly through the world in powerful ways that elude the notion of boldly writ cause and effect. Relevance does not always stride through the world trailing banners of fame and fortune. Daniel and Dora Salk had little formal education, but they were fiercely determined to see their children succeed. The world may not remember Dora's name, but she encouraged her son Jonas to forgo law in favor of a medical career. We will never know whether, in the absence of Dora's influence, Jonas Salk would have developed the vaccine to combat the scourge of polio.

Throughout history, there have been people who mattered more. Some of them, like Ulysses S. Grant and Winston Churchill and Jonas Salk, changed the course of history in grand strokes. Others, like Reuben Styrlund and Dora Salk, made a meaningful difference on a smaller stage. Our lives are marked by the people who choose to matter more: the teacher who encourages our curiosity, the neighbor who lends a helping hand in time of need, the great leaders and perceptive thinkers whose vision and innovation improve the quality of our lives. And that's what it means to matter more. It's not about the pursuit of riches or fame. It's about making a difference in people's lives. Remembered or not, lived out in a small town or on the world's stage, the journey of relevance matters.

Reuben Styrlund's desire to matter started us on this exploration of what it means to live a relevant life. Reuben lived well and ended well. He passed to us his passion for mattering more. We share it with you. We are all companions on this road to relevance, and we hope our thoughts and observations are of value to you on your journey. We look forward to continuing the conversation, to sharing thoughts and experiences and ideas that will help us to matter more to each other, and for each other, in the time that is given to us.

BIOGRAPHIES

PHIL STYRLUND

As CEO of The Summit Group, Phil is a recognized thought leader on sales transformation and development as part of the go-to-market strategies of some of the world's premier organizations in the public and private sectors, including Cisco, Xerox, General Mills, Marriott, 3M, Medtronic, Pfizer, Abbott, and U.S. federal government agencies. In addition to keynotes and training programs delivered in more than 45 countries, Phil serves as a coach, mentor, consultant, and advisor to top leaders across a range of industries. Recently, Phil was elected to the board of directors for SAMA (Strategic Account Management Association). He also leads the CEO Forum as part of the annual National Prayer Breakfast in Washington, D.C.

Phil has written for, or been cited in, articles in leading publications that include: *The Wall Street Journal*, the *National Account Management Journal*, the *Los Angeles Times, Inc.*, and *Fast Company*, as well as in several best-selling books, including *Adversity Quotient* and *The Power of Purpose*.

His career includes key leadership positions with US West and ADC Telecommunications. Phil also teaches in various university and executive education programs, and has master's degrees in business administration and telecommunications science. He recently initiated a doctoral program at Middlesex University in London.

Phil resides in Minneapolis, Minnesota, and Santa Barbara, California.

summitvalue.com

TOM HAYES

Tom Hayes is the founder and owner of Riley Hayes, an advertising agency now in its third decade. Having started his advertising career as a copywriter, Tom has now returned to his love of writing with *Relevance: Matter More*. He has put the book's principles to use throughout his business, applying them to employee and agency evaluations, and using them in creative briefs, new business pitches, and strategic planning. As a result, Riley Hayes is recognized for work that helps client brands and products matter more to their customers, achieving relevant results. The agency is honored to serve some of America's most prestigious clients, including Delta Air Lines, U.S. Bank, Walgreens, 3M, Allen Edmonds, Alerus Financial, Tradition Capital Bank, Korn Ferry, Scholarship America, and Dunn Bros Coffee. Tom takes particular pride in the ways Riley Hayes has been able to help clients, large and small, enjoy sustainable success.

Tom's thoughts on relevance, advertising, and marketing are published in a variety of publications and websites, and can be found on Tom's site, tomhayesmattermore.com. In addition to his agency leadership and writing, Tom shares his thinking about the principles of *Relevance: Matter More* through speaking engagements and strategic planning sessions.

Tom's avocations include helping underserved communities move forward, supporting underserved youth in the pursuit of higher education, and spending as much time as he can in nature. Tom is blessed with a large, loving, Irish-American family, including his wife, Sheila, and adult children Katie, Pat, and Ryan. Tom lives in Shorewood, Minnesota, a short walk from his family's ancestral home.

rileyhayes.com | tomhayesmattermore.com

MARIAN DEEGAN

As the founder of Fortuni, Marian writes for business and health care innovators. Her work is grounded in more than 20 years of national advertising experience and is informed by multidisciplinary credentials in law, philosophy, and the arts. Marian understands the subtle intangibles that bring the facts to life in her profiles of CEOs, surgeons, and community leaders. She is a contributing writer and editor for the Immunization Action Coalition and *MD News-Minnesota*, and a lecturer and consultant on business writing. Marian is committed to client collaborations that support thoughtful, healthy, and inspired communities.

fortuni.com